Original Sin

Original Sin

From Preacher's Kid to
the Creation of CinemaSins
and 3.5+ Billion Views

JEREMY SCOTT

TURNER
PUBLISHING COMPANY

Turner Publishing Company
Nashville, Tennessee

www.turnerpublishing.com

Original Sin

Copyright © 2021 by Jeremy Scott. All rights reserved.

Cover design: Lauren Peters-Collaer
Book design: Tim Holtz

9781684425532   Paperback
9781684425549   Hardback
9781684425556   Ebook

Printed in the United States of America

This book is dedicated first to my mom and dad.
We haven't always seen eye-to-eye on life... or movies.
But I have never doubted their love for me and their desire
to see me succeed. I am grateful to them for the positive
qualities they instilled in me. Additionally I would like to
dedicate this book to anyone that has ever loved movies;
we all come to movies from different backgrounds and
histories, but the common denominator is the ability
for a movie to transport a person to another reality,
even if only temporarily. May the movies never die.

CONTENTS

FOREWORD

(Jeremy asked a few of the folks who know him best to each write a small foreword about Jeremy and movies. All but one agreed . . . fucking Trevor.)

Jeff Scott – Jeremy's brother

When your little brother becomes "internet famous" overnight, it creates some self-esteem issues. When he asks you to write a foreword for yet another book he is having published, well, now he's just rubbing it in. Born two years apart and growing up in a series of small rural communities, Jeremy and I spent most of our time together, because honestly, there weren't that many other options. We were either the closest of friends or the bitterest of enemies, often in the same afternoon.

As you will read in the following pages, our parents didn't take us to movies when we were growing up, primarily due to our father being a pastor and our church being weirdly neurotic about movies and dancing and blue jeans for some reason. When I left for college, I jumped into the deep end. In my first year away from home, I saw many of what I still consider to be my favorite films of all time: *The Silence of the Lambs*, *Terminator 2*, *Beauty and the Beast*, *The Fisher King*, *What About Bob* ("I'll

be peace!"), *Barton Fink, The Commitments,* and *Rosencrantz &*
Guildenstern Are Dead, among others. Okay, so my grades may
have suffered, and I might have lost my scholarship, but that's
clearly on my parents, right?

Whenever I came home for a visit, I did what any self-
respecting big brother would do—I took my brother to the
movies. I don't remember asking permission, but he didn't seem
to mind. And I guess he got hooked. A couple of decades and
millions of subscribers later and, well, you're welcome. Or I'm
sorry. I'm still not sure myself.

Movies aren't real life, but they help us make sense of real
life. They get our creative juices flowing and allow us to develop
opinions about beauty and art and truth. They make us feel
things we didn't know we needed to feel and give us an accept-
able excuse to feel them. They permit us to laugh and cry and
scream at ourselves in manageable chunks of time.

Jeremy and I are still close, and we still go to the movies
together. We still argue. He's still wrong about a few films, and,
as his big brother, I'm still right about pretty much everything.
But he is also the most relentlessly creative person I've ever
known, and thankfully, you don't have to take my word for it.
You can read his books (start with this one—I wrote one of
the forewords!), subscribe to any of the numerous YouTube
channels or podcasts he's helped create, or just follow him on
Twitter for a few days. I'm confident, like the movies, he'll
make you laugh or cry or scream. Probably all three. And who
knows? Maybe he will help you get your own creative juices
flowing.

Thanks for coming to my TED Talk.

Chris Atkinson – Jeremy's friend and the cofounder of CinemaSins

While I have known Jeremy since 1999 when we worked together at the Hollywood 27 movie theater in Nashville, one of my earliest memories of him was in January of 2001, when *Save the Last Dance* hit screens.

You should realize that people who work in movie theaters and get to watch movies during off-hours have it way, way better than the commoners. You get a whole auditorium to yourself and occasionally your coworkers, you can load up on free soft drinks and popcorn, and you can say stuff to the screen that would get you (rightfully) ejected during regularly scheduled shows.

Jeremy and I, both followers of *Mystery Science Theater 3000*, would often say things in direct response to the actions and dialogue on-screen. Many of these things are wholly inappropriate, and one of those things Jeremy said has stuck with me for almost twenty years—nothing he'd have to formally apologize for, but certainly over the line. Anyway, both of us just happened to be doing this MST3K stuff during a screening where our concessions manager and others were present, and at some point, one of them turned around and said, "Do you have to talk through the entire movie?"

I guess we were ruining movies for people even then. Also, we replied, "Yes."

While the main criticism of CinemaSins is that we "hate movies," you should realize that nobody who hates movies would even watch *Save the Last Dance*. Those people certainly wouldn't make fun of movies in a way that extends beyond, "This movie sucks." People like Jeremy give movies a chance that the public at large doesn't. You'll find his love for movies that weren't even released in theaters that he's seen more than twice. Try asking anybody on the street if they've seen *Wrong Turn 5: Bloodlines*, much less loved it. I mean, don't try just going out on the street and asking this question to pedestrians—that's what a crazy person does. But I'm certain if you find one person who's like, "Yeah, I LOVE that movie," there's a 100 percent chance you stumbled upon Jeremy himself.

I don't know if that totally explains (forgives? justifies?) CinemaSins on the whole, but it should give you a clearer idea of why it exists.

Josh Childs – Jeremy's friend since college and old writing buddy

Movies are the thing. It's nearly impossible to disassociate movies from hanging out with Jer. Sneaking out of boring events to go catch movies. Hanging outside of Blockbuster on his cigarette break to talk about movies. Getting in free, when he worked at the theater, to watch movies. Even my bachelor party was, thanks to him being the manager, hanging out in the theater all night watching movies. There's a post-college, pre-marriage sweet spot for some, where roommates meander through life, skirting any major responsibilities. Most of my best memories of this era involve Jer and movies. But I want to go back even further.

Our friendship was a legacy, in a way. Both of our older brothers met in college and bonded over movies, so when we attended the same college, that bond was handed down. In a conservative Christian college, where the Nazarene denomination believed (at that point) that going to movies was a sin, this was an especially unique bond. (The school also took issue with students wearing shorts to class, but my legs are really skinny and hairy, so I'll leave that commentary for some other ex-Nazarene, writing a foreword for a different friend and collaborator, working on a different kind of book.)

I don't want to give the impression that Jer and I were some poor, huddled, moviegoing holdouts in a totalitarian regime. I believe most of the students who attended the college casually attended the theater, but we were obsessed. Movies were more than casual entertainment. Watching wasn't enough. I think I can speak for both of us when I say we were desperately looking for a way to crawl inside them . . . to wear them like some sort of thick girl skin, or maybe an Edgar suit . . .

Speaking of Edgar suit, we wrote *Men in Black*. Well, almost. Well, we considered it . . . Neither of us had read the graphic novel, so we had no awareness that this franchise was already in motion. In fact, when we set out to write our version, the tone of our story was probably more in line with a *Trancers* sequel than a blockbuster extravaganza (I'm sure this was my fault, since Jer didn't generally watch movies that aimed right for the middle . . . or bottom). We decided to get serious about it. I recall a writer's retreat he and I took to work on the script. I remember eating Mexican food, smoking more expensive cigarettes than normal, and watching movies on cable all night. When the trip was over, all we really had was a few pages and some funny characters (Was someone named Basil . . . ? After the spice . . . ? Okay, maybe the characters weren't that funny).

Less mainstream (and predating the retreat), we also wrote

Coffee and Cigarettes before Jarmusch ever shared his sit-y down-y talky series of vignettes.

Bray's was a twenty-four-hour diner far enough away from campus to smoke without getting caught (for fear of fines . . . or worse, condemnation to Hell) but close enough to get there and back before curfew (again, to avoid fines and Hell). There were a few of us who would go periodically to, you guessed it, smoke cigarettes and drink coffee. When Jer and I went, we always brought a notebook. This was our ongoing "Diner Theater" script. We just wrote conversations that characters might be having over coffee and cigarettes.

"What if the cast of *City Slickers* reunited for a sequel on the ocean, and it was called *Land Lubbers*?"

"Only if Jack Palance came back as Curley's curmudgeonly twin brother sea captain."

Brilliant stuff like that. (See! Even our scripts were about movies.) For a while we thought, "Hey, maybe we'll film these." But we decided that probably every writer and/or film student had already tried this, and it was probably a pretentious, self-gratifying exercise that nobody would find interesting but us. After watching *Coffee and Cigarettes*, I think we made the right choice.

Over twenty-five years later, we're both still obsessed with movies. I don't know that I learned a lot about the actual craft of screenwriting or filmmaking from those early endeavors, but I learned a lot about collaboration, and that I wasn't alone in my obsessive nerdery (remember, this was way before film Twitter). Over twenty-five years later, when we hang out, topics of conversation always include "Have you seen anything good lately?"

and/or "I have another idea for a movie." And anyone who watches CinemaSins, listens to the podcasts, hangs out with his friends and coworkers, or even meets Jer knows that all of it points to the fact that he's still trying to crawl inside that mystical anomaly of film like it's Malkovich's brain, or Godzilla's suit, or Ethan Hunt's rubber mask, or the Matrix, or . . .

Aaron Dicer – Jeremy's friend since college and old bowling buddy

Here's what you need to know about Jeremy Scott.

We're the same person.

I don't mean literally the same person—or maybe I do, believe what you want, I'm not your dad, or maybe I am . . . but I digress.

We were born in May of 1975 in the Midwest. Our dad was a Nazarene pastor, a minor protestant denomination with well-defined guidelines on what it meant to live a "Holy" life. We found our love of performing and entertainment inside the walls of our church and our love of movies despite the walls of our church. In the fall of 1993 we found our way to a denominational school just south of Chicago and were singled out as one of two freshmen guys to participate in the annual talent show. We didn't win. We did, however, join the radio program, perform with a college singing group, star in the production of *Diary of Anne Frank*, and wonder why nobody else loved *Sneakers*, *Quiz Show*, or *The Hudsucker Proxy* quite as much as we did. Those same passions one day led us to quit our day jobs to focus on content creation through YouTube, podcasting, and writing.

What I'm trying to say is that this book must be awesome, because I wrote it.

And also because you wrote it too.

Sure, you may not have the exact same origin, upbringing, or history with film, but I'm convinced you'll see your own laughter, passion, ambition, and heart printed on almost every page. In my time with Jer, whether it be standing above the Cumberland on Nashville's pedestrian bridge chatting *The Wire*, hurling snark at an early screening of *Volcano*, or discussing where we stood in relation to the faith of our childhood, I always felt welcome, I always had a good time, and I always connected deeply. And I would be shocked if you didn't feel the same way reading this.

Because here's the thing you need to know about this book: I'm in it ...

... and so are you.

Barrett Share – Jeremy's friend and cohost of the CinemaSins podcast, the *SinCast*

The first movie that I specifically remember watching in the theater with Jeremy was *The Wolf of Wall Street* in 2013. But I'd been watching movies "with" him for much longer than that. Not only was he likely the projectionist for many films I'd seen at his various theaters in Nashville, but it turns out that we have extremely similar tastes and may have been watching the same movie, at the very same time, in different places, for years before we even met.

From the very beginning of our friendship, we spoke to each other with cinematic verbiage. We both were fans of silly comedies, sleek sci-fi, and super-smart actioners, so there was endless material to discuss. For the last four years we've been doing the same thing formally on our weekly podcast, but the movie talk doesn't end there. It carries on through meals, drinks, and off-the-cuff kitchen chat.

There's a level of cinematic ponderance that's deep and rich without being pretentious, and I think that's how Jeremy thinks about movies. He always has a fresh perspective that makes me see things in a new light, whether that's good, bad, or silly. And trust me . . . it can be silly. Whenever I write with him on a project, his material will murder me at LEAST a few times when I read it.

I'm happy to have worked with Jeremy for this long, but our friendship has lasted even longer and is much more important to me. He's also a terrific cook, so if he bribes you into helping him with a project with the promise of grilled meat, I suggest you accept.

Jason Elkins – Jeremy's friend, lunch buddy, and occasional conscience

Knowing Jeremy Scott for more than a decade has been one of my life's joys. We worked together in a previous job, and I have always been in awe of his work ethic and his creativity.

Our company tasked him with writing a weekly blog. He would crank through one in minutes. When it was my turn to submit an article, it would be days or weeks before I could produce something I was proud of, but Jeremy would just rip through them in less than an hour, and they were really well written.

After we stopped working for the same company, I was able to witness the building of CinemaSins. He and Chris made really funny videos, but I was blown away by the consistency and their ability to produce them so quickly. I asked him one time for the magic formula for his YouTube success and he said, "I don't know, man, we just created these videos we thought were funny, and then we didn't stop."

It wasn't long after CinemaSins took off that the books started coming. I got to read an early version of *The Ables* with my then-young teens. We all loved it and couldn't wait for the next books to come out!

I've always been a fan of movies, but Jeremy possesses a deep understanding of cinema and has introduced me to incredible shows I would have never found on my own. *The Raid 2, Bad Times at the El Royale, The Town,* and *Snowpiercer* are just a few movies he insisted on me seeing. My wife will forgive him at some point for the scene in *Snowpiercer* where the train workers find out the food they're eating is made from bugs (Ding!).

To challenge his knowledge, we have an ongoing game we play where I text him a picture of a show or movie I'm watching. He has to guess what it is. I never make it easy. I'll simply show a picture of the main actor or actress or a secondary character, and he replies with an answer. We've been doing this for a few years, and I can count on one hand the times he's been incorrect. Jeremy's knowledge of movies is astounding.

If you're lucky to have a true friend or two in your lifetime, you've won. If that friend knows all of the best movies to see, that's like a real-life "bonus round." Who knows ... They just might be excellent at CinemaSins.

PROLOGUE

I can't believe you actually bought this book.

Did you fall for all the flowery words and humorous stories my friends told you in the foreword?! Classic mistake. Never trust the author of a book's foreword—they are already bought and paid for. I bought Jeff a fucking Jet Ski, for Christ's sake, and he lives in Ohio!

Look, I am going to level with you. Most of this is just a humorous memoir about how I met Chris and started and grew CinemaSins into a full-time job. If you're only here for action-able advice regarding YouTube, because you really do want to know what we did that we think helped our success so that you can repeat those things, I did include a chapter just for you.

It's chapter 11, and if all you're looking for is the advice I would give to any upstart new YouTube channel, then feel free to skip ahead and get your money's worth. But I'll warn you, all the stuff you're skipping over is fucking hilarious. Your loss, Mr. Fame-Chaser Man. Or Woman.

The most common factor in YouTube success that people take for granted is luck. Blind, dumb, lucky fucking luck.

For instance, our first video, "Everything Wrong With *The Amazing Spider-Man*," ended up on the home page of Buzzfeed.

We didn't do that. We couldn't have done that if we wanted to. But it was a huge part of the reason our channel found early success—literally our first video ever got viral views from a massively popular landing spot on the web.

So many of my well-intentioned friends have, post Cinema-Sins, decided they should also try making a living on YouTube. But when their videos don't go viral, they come to me wondering why. Like it had been so easy for me that they couldn't fathom their own failure.

Never mind that one of them was posting videos with Canadian Football League analysis, or that another was doing a video podcast about various lesser-known uses for corn. It was my fault their channels weren't succeeding. I hadn't given them good enough pointers.

It was a great time of misunderstanding. It was early 2013, and I was making money on YouTube videos, working from home. Our only overhead at the time was the cost of each Blu-ray disc.

I'll never forget going to check my mail in mid-2013, after YouTube had become my full-time job, and running into my neighbor from across the street checking his mail at the same time.

He was old and friendly and reminded me of Santa Claus. "I hope you find work again soon," he said, sincerely enough, before walking back up his driveway.

That old man cared enough to spy on me and notice that I never left the house, at least not at traditional "person who has a job" times. And he was concerned enough about my income that he wanted me to know he was concerned.

Which, I mean . . . nosy much, Santa?

We did wait to quit our other jobs, I'll be honest. We gathered subscribers quickly and had nearly one hundred thousand in a few months, but we were wary of the whole thing. We waited to leave other employment until we got checks from YouTube for a few solid months. Finally it felt real and not like a pipe dream.

By mid-2013, we were both working full-time on Cinema-Sins stuff and working from home.

The rest is history.

Today we have four full-time employees beyond Chris and I, which means six full-time CinemaSins peeps. We have offshoot channels like TVSins and MusicVideoSins, bringing our total YouTube audience to eleven million subscribers and growing. And CommercialSins recently launched!

Our Patreon continues to grow, and our podcast gets over two hundred thousand downloads per month. We're talking about a cooking channel, and suddenly we are your everyday accidental twenty-first-century media brand, making it up as we go.

Making it up as we go . . . could be a CinemaSins slogan, or a subtitle for this book!

Is CinemaSins comedy? Yes. Is it criticism? Sometimes. Should it be taken seriously? Only by people who get the joke.

And this book here . . . is it a memoir? Kind of. Is it a humor book? Yeah, a bit. Is it an instructional tome? Here and there.

Look, I figure . . . you're on the second page of the prologue and still reading. Why bother defining it or picking a genre? You already bought it. What do I care?

Anyway, thanks for your money.

CHAPTER 1

Everything Starts Somewhere

I was born not breathing, and for two minutes the doctors worked to revive me. Eventually I choked back to life, and ever since then I have been celebrated in my family as a miracle child. The kid who wasn't breathing. It's family lore.

Actually . . . none of that is true. That's my brother's story. He was born two and a half years before me, and yes, he was born not breathing.

My own birth was normal and inconsequential.

I guess I just wanted to open this book with a bang.

I'm sorry. It probably does nothing to build goodwill with the readers if I'm stealing stories this early on in the book, right? Yeah, I can't pull off the evil con man Artful Dodger type any better than I can pull off the totally innocent Oliver type.

Hmm.

What if I told you I didn't care so much about goodwill once I'd gotten your money?

Not better? Okay. Moving on.

Anyway ... I was born in May of 1975, in Kansas City, Missouri.

My birth included no special circumstances to relay. Nothing unique about me. This was only of note because, of course, my older brother had been born not breathing and then had been revived, as I said ... like a miracle. My beginning was like being born to Mary and Joseph *after* they'd had Jesus.

Or to Mr. and Mrs. Pitt *after* they'd given birth to Brad.

Anyway, two weeks after I was born, we moved from the Midwest to Baltimore, Maryland. This is where I came of age and learned to talk and walk and appreciate baseball. Oriole baseball, of course.

My love of baseball started when I was very young and lines up nicely with my exposure to baseball.

Baseball was considered a family-friendly sport in the late '70s and early '80s. My parents, who were stricter than most, allowed me to not only watch baseball on television but also to go to games with them at Memorial Park.

My family's favorite story to tell about me is that I fell asleep at Memorial Park during an Orioles game, but when the house organ played the notes calling for us to yell "Charge!", I yelled "Charge!" even in my sleep.

But obsession can grow out of early exposure or from early and constant denial. Which is how I became obsessed with movies.

The Nazarene denomination wasn't a big fan of Hollywood and movies back in the late '70s. It was seen as a place where the Devil's ideas incubated and sprang forth toward unsuspecting youths.

Going to a movie theater was about like going to a strip club or a casino in the eyes of my father's particular brand of Protestantism.

And if you tell a small child enough times over that he can't or shouldn't do a thing . . . that child starts to want to do the thing. It's odd to me that most every generation of parents fails to learn this lesson.

So from middle school on, I wanted nothing more than to watch movies . . . to go to the cinema . . . to buy the popcorn and overpriced soda . . . to sit among noisy strangers . . . I wanted the full experience. But I would only have it a few times before turning eighteen.

Chris Atkinson and I met in the spring of 1999, the opening weekend of *The Phantom Menace*. I'd been working for the Regal Cinemas Hollywood 27 in Nashville as a manager since April. It was a step up for me from my assistant manager job at a Blockbuster Video. I'd been an assistant manager at a smaller chain of movie theaters prior to the Blockbuster job, which I really only took because it was literally three blocks from my house at the time and I had an unreliable car.

The Phantom Menace was an interesting time for movie theater employees. It was the first new *Star Wars* film in nearly twenty years, so it created lines around the building, customers in costume, and a host of other previously unforeseen movie theater problems.

Among the issues surrounding the release of *The Phantom Menace* was a list of theater employee rules sent out by Lucasfilm. And the rules were fucking insane.

Like, you know how ushers sometimes come into your movie and walk up and down the aisles and stairs? They're checking for loud patrons, people screwing, feet up on chairs, or any other anomalies in the auditorium.

Lucasfilm wanted all ushers doing safety walks of auditoriums to do so with their backs constantly facing the screen so as to avoid them seeing the film without paying. All our auditoriums were stadium seating, so ushers would have had to have backed all the way down the stairs without tripping . . . if we'd followed those dumbass rules. We did not.

The company also asked theater chains to black out the film for early employee screenings—a Thursday night perk of the job for decades. That one we had to follow because . . . reasons.

Another concern Lucasfilm had was piracy. So we'd been told to be on the lookout for people videotaping the movie. And I was standing in projection looking through that little window, trying to figure out if this dude in the middle of the audience had a camcorder or just a bright watch.

And that's when I met Chris. He and our district manager were walking down the projection hall behind me, and we were introduced.

One of the early things that we bonded over was just good projection skills. Most employees in the booth were manager/projectionists. Which meant most of them saw a shift in the booth the same way they saw one in concession: just another task.

Chris and I actually cared about good projection work like building a clean print, maintaining the lamp to keep brightness levels consistent, and cleaning the machines regularly. It mattered to us that people got a good presentation, because before we'd worked at movie theaters . . . we were those people in there.

The next thing we bonded over was shouting jokes at the screen during Thursday night screenings.

One of the great perks of the job as a projectionist is that if you built a movie, you had to—HAD TO—watch that movie to make sure there were no mistakes in the build or scratches on the film.

Now, this was around 2000 or so, back when they still used film. These days most theaters you go to are using digital projectors and digital movie files. It doesn't really change the experience, and in some ways it improves it, but there was an art to building a solid print of a movie from six or seven reels. And now that art is largely dying out.

Anyway, every Thursday night, Chris and I would watch movies that one or both of us had built, sometimes watching two or three movies until the wee hours of the morning.

We didn't mind; we loved movies!

We'd both seen *Mystery Science Theater 3000* and were big fans, and it just became a natural thing for us to joke aloud while we watched a movie together.

This was years before YouTube would even be invented, and even more years before we would create a channel, but this time in our lives was undeniably the seed of what would eventually become CinemaSins.

I remember a double feature night of *Jeepers Creepers* and *O*—the Julia Stiles modern *Othello* movie. A lot of the best jokes that night are too dirty for even this R-rated book.

I remember the night before *Scream 3* came out, and I

decided to move a print of the film all on my own. Moving a print on your own is always a bad idea, but so is speeding, and we all do that anyway, right?

Moving *Scream 3* alone was a super bad idea because it was a large print, and it wasn't quite as tight around the ring as it should have been. So, of course, I dropped the fucking thing. Six reels of film on the floor in what I liked to call a "salad."

Everyone else got to enjoy *Scream 3* that night.

Well, I guess I'm using the word "enjoy" loosely since *Scream 3* is fucking terrible.

But I didn't get to watch it, because I had to clean up my mess. This meant following the film, cutting and reattaching it in several places to fix tangles, and generally some of the most frustrating work you can do for two hours.

But even though I messed up and dropped the film, and that shouldn't have happened, I still took a weird pride in carefully putting the film back together with minimal scratches.

There was a section of about maybe sixty-five frames or so that, unfortunately, I couldn't salvage, resulting in a pretty hilariously important three seconds of the film's climax being completely jumped over. Oops.

Projectionists like to take pride in great booth achievements. Things like building five movies in a single shift. Chris has some wild stories about interlocking—taking one copy of the film and threading it through multiple projectors at once. It's often tricky, because any malfunction in equipment shuts down ALL the auditoriums showing that print of the film.

My big brag was the Saturday afternoon so many other managers called out that I had to run the entire booth myself.

Twenty-seven projectors for twenty-seven different auditoriums. Typically this was split between two projectionists on each shift, and even then it could sometimes be a hustle, depending on the actual show times.

I wasn't the only guy to run all twenty-seven for a shift, but I was one of only a few, and it was pretty exhausting work. But I was proud of it.

It helped that my and Chris's tastes in film were similar and largely overlapping. We shared a similar affinity for sarcasm. We both loved sports.

And so we became friends. He served in my wedding party; we invited each other to Oscar parties and NCAA Tournament parties. We both loved U2 a little more than is reasonable. I actually remember a night we worked the late shift together and were both excited to go to Media Play at the other end of the strip mall at midnight when the *Beautiful Day* album launched.

Ha ha ha ha ha ha ha ha ha . . . Media Play.

For a few hazy years we went to a weekly bar trivia event, drank too much beer, then moved bars to play darts for a few hours, and I swear to God Jakob Dylan was there one night playing darts next to us, and he was *tiny*.

Anyway, I got married and decided to get out of the theater management profession, mostly due to the weird and many hours required.

While Chris kept providing excellent film presentation at various theaters, including a stint in New York City, I worked in online marketing, helping clients rank well on Google via SEO—search engine optimization. Be careful who you say that phrase around, because there are groups of happily ignorant people that believe SEO is inherently shady. It's not. It's the most basic and simplest thing. Put the keywords you want to rank for naturally on your website—use the text and the headings—and that's most of the work.

My customers were local small businesses, so it wasn't difficult to get them ranking well.

There *are* some SEO people out there that do engage in shady practices like buying links or tricking the search engines. So SEO is like any other profession. Most people in it are doing their jobs and are above board, but of course there are shady dickheads that cheat.

As YouTube was released and grew in popularity, I went to work for ReelSEO.com, a website that specialized in news and tips for video marketing online, including video SEO. Again, keywords. Use keywords. (Learn more in chapter 11, the Actionable Advice chapter.)

After a while, Chris joined me as another writer on the site, and we both went on to serve as editor of ReelSEO before leaving to pursue video-making full-time.

Reporting on YouTube's early superstars like Freddie Wong and Hannah Hart gave us the itch to make our own videos. We were creative. We were funny. We were FUNNY—I see you rolling your eyes, guy who hate-bought this book. We're funny! Get over it.

None of the viewers of our first channel thought we were remotely funny.

The concept was to review films well before their release and pretend we'd seen them. We made up ridiculous details about the films, and we always acted surprised to see the Bruce Willis cameo—which was a gag for every "review" video.

Our second channel had more success. We created a series of supercuts. Our supercuts were all the most repetitive things we could find about a particular movie or franchise. We started by cutting down *Pulp Fiction* to just the cussing. That video got some traction and plenty of views, and we were pleased.

The next one we tried was "*Kickboxer*: Just the Kicking." Then "*Harry Potter*: Just the Spells," and "*Fast & Furious*: Just the gear shifting!" You could guess a few of the others, I bet. Several of them did quite well, but the subscribers never increased much, and we weren't able to monetize the videos.

Eventually we started getting copyright claims, and You-Tube threatened to kill the channel, so we had to delete most of those videos.

And boy was I angry. I was livid.

I knew that supercuts were very likely something that would fall under Fair Use as far as copyright was concerned. But I didn't have anyone backing me on YouTube—no management company or anything. I had no way to plead my case.

I vowed to come up with a type of video that used movie footage but changed and added enough to it that it would be more clearly a case of Fair Use. And that's literally how Cinema-Sins was born.

My email to Chris was: "What if it's a know-it-all, like *The Simpsons*'s comic book nerd, pointing out all the flaws in a movie, but with the rapid delivery of those old Micro Machines commercials?"

We decided to use the word "sins" instead of "flaws" so that the label could be more broadly applied and less easy to define as any one thing. "Movie sins?" I asked, to which Chris replied, "Definitely cinema sins; go with the alliteration."

A week later *The Amazing Spider-Man* sins video was complete. Instead of titling the video "The Sins of *The Amazing Spider-Man*," we went with the more incendiary opening of "Everything Wrong With." That has proven to be an obstacle to a lot of potential viewers understanding what it is we're really trying to do. But it's also been a huge boost to our views, because—as we suspected—the all-negative tone of the title proved quite good at starting conversations and debates in the comments, on social media, and beyond.

By the second video, one of my favorite Uproxx sites declared that CinemaSins had "overstayed its welcome" in just a single week. That's good coverage, baby. I ain't even joking.

In fact, every time a major publication has posted an article critical of our channel . . . every time a famous person has used social media to decry CinemaSins . . . every single time, our subscriptions spiked to levels five to ten times higher than average. I mean, it still hurt, especially if we respected the celebrity or the publication, but it still was good for business.

There was one time one guy got so mad he tweeted about us nearly sixty times in twenty-four hours. I could show you a subscriber-count chart from that week, and it would blow your mind how many new fans we gained, despite the new non-fans we also gained.

But I'm getting ahead of myself.

Well, I'm also going too slowly.

This is going to be an experimental book, where I tell

stories from the past when Chris and I worked in movie theaters together concurrent with stories from the recent past about CinemaSins and YouTube and our experiences after the channel's success. Not to mention the stories from my preacher's-kid youth.

I'm going to go back and forth a lot, and I honestly don't want to take the time to put everything in chronological order.

I want this book to feel like an actual conversation with me: meandering and mostly filler.

I'm kidding. There's no filler.

But the meandering thing was true. Just read the next chapter to find out what I mean.

CHAPTER 2

Famous People React

My dad had a simple rule about movie theaters: don't go to them. So, for the most part, I did not. A few times Mom or a friend's mom would talk Dad into letting me go to the movies. So I saw *The Black Cauldron*, *The Care Bears Movie*, and *Return of the Jedi*.

When I was sixteen, I went to see *A Few Good Men*, and my friend lost his wallet. His mother worked at the church where my dad was pastor, and I was busted. I remember getting the "as long as you're living under our roof" speech.

Point is, the only movies I saw for most of my first eighteen years were borrowed from the library and father-approved for content. I was allowed to see some movies. But not anything edgy or R-rated. Nothing in an actual cinema.

By the time I got to college I was like Fred Flintstone, having spun my feet for a good while before peeling out in my pursuit of any and every movie I could see. Within six months I was an assistant manager at a theater, and I worked in movie theaters for the next eight or nine years. I left three times and kept coming right back. The theater business gets into your blood. Or under your skin, rather.

Working at a theater—and especially in the booth where you handled the film and machinery that made the "magic" of the silver screen happen—was as close as any of us would ever get to being in the actual film industry.

There's a romance to working at a theater, even if it is often obscured by people vomiting, horrible customers, terrible bosses, and the smell of cigarettes. I haven't done the math exactly, but at least nine out of every ten theater workers smokes cigarettes. I did too. I don't anymore, but that's another story for another time.

When Chris and I worked together, the theater was among the busiest in the mid-state. We sometimes had celebrities come to see a film, like Ashley Judd, Jewel, Tom Hanks, and Eddie George of the Tennessee Titans, whose calves were as round as my waist.

Once in a blue moon we got some kind of mid-south movie premiere event. I know Bob Seger was in the building for *Black Dog*, and I wasn't there, but Jeremy Piven and some others brought a car salesman movie to the theater for a premiere.

But Hollywood, and the people working in it, were still celebrities to us. A different class of people and certainly not people we would ever meet or hear from.

And then CinemaSins launched.

The first celebrity that I'm aware of who tweeted about our videos was Kevin Smith. He was a fan and tweeted out our

YouTube page to his insane number of followers. We got a swell of subscribers for weeks from that one mention. We owe him a great deal of thanks and some sexual acts.

Dane Cook, most notable to me for his supporting turn in the underappreciated *Mr. Brooks*, also tweeted out his affection for our videos. I think he had two million followers at that point.

Eventually we managed to get negative feedback, and it was Rian Johnson, who didn't quite appreciate our video about his film *Looper*, even though he did seem to understand that we weren't being serious.

This event was the entire reason we even created a Twitter account, and we replied that we were just assholes joking around.

On one hand, it sucks, because we really respect his work as a filmmaker. We both loved *Looper*, and *Brick* and *The Lookout* before that, as well as Johnson's episodes of *Breaking Bad*.

But on the other hand, I also understand that when you make something and pour your heart into it, it's not always fun or easy to hear a long list of criticisms, even ones that aren't intended to be taken seriously.

A lot of the people who don't like CinemaSins, celebrity or not, simply haven't spent much time watching our videos—not that they should. But if you read the title "everything wrong with" over and over, you develop an idea of what that channel's videos are.

But from the very first video ever, a percentage of our "sins" have always been so ridiculous as to serve as signal flares for anyone thinking the videos are meant to be taken seriously.

The first video had us giving one particular sin to *The Amazing Spider-Man* because Uncle Ben picked up a Rubik's Cube and set it down without solving it. Now, how can you think we're making a serious critique of the movie when we say that?

And I guess that's the joke ... at least for me. That most of our haters don't understand that we are making fun of the very thing they think we are. If we were being serious with our lists and our videos, then yes ... we would be terrible people and would deserve scorn.

Another filmmaker and writer I respect, Damon Lindelof, tweeted about our *Dark Knight* video. I don't think he knew that we were doing a shtick, and I think he just saw the video being passed around online, so he thought we were just being mean to a great movie. And we were, I guess. But we were doing it for fun.

Anyone who thinks CinemaSins hates movies needs only to listen to one full episode of our podcast to see who we really are. And that's a bunch of film-loving friends that like to talk. And cuss. We cuss a lot. Get the fuck over it. Again, not that you *should* listen to our podcast. But if you think we hate movies, there is plenty of evidence to suggest otherwise if you are willing to take a look, or a listen.

Which is also how I hope the director of a certain ape movie feels as well. He tweeted at or about us nearly sixty times inside twenty-four hours. He was angry, and that's okay. He spent years working on a project he cared deeply about, and then we spent a few days making a video tearing it to pieces.

Anyway, as his tirade continued, fans of ours stepped in to tell him we were satire, and much of the tweeting turned to the definition of satire.

And first of all, I never said we were satire. We never defended ourselves publicly as satire.

I could make a case that we *are* satire, which Google tells me is defined as:

The use of humor, irony, exaggeration, or ridicule to expose and criticize people's stupidity or vices, particularly in the context of contemporary politics and other topical issues.

That could easily be applied to our content, but apparently there are online warriors for the word "satire" who defend it from wrongful use and are quite insistent on a more rigid definition.

To those people I say: we never said that. We would not have used that word. We would maybe have said parody. Or an exaggeration. No one on Team Sins is trying to invoke "satire."

We are and always have been playing a character. A character that believes he has the most and best knowledge about all films, and his opinions are always correct. Everyone has someone like this in their circle—sometimes it's about sports and not film. Think about that person. They are always a know-it-all. They are often obnoxious and loud. They are often wrong about things they insist they are right about. But sometimes they're also right, which only makes them even more annoying.

THAT is who makes the Sins videos. He's a character.

If you didn't know that before now, now you know. We always thought it was obvious. But it clearly is not. We show our love of movies and celebrate it together through over-the-top observation and nitpicking for the sake of humor. We never expected everyone would find it funny, but we also never expected people to take us seriously.

But as for the director behind the sixty-plus tweets? That dude later went to Vietnam for vacation—or maybe location scouting, I don't quite remember—and a bunch of random dudes jumped him in a bar and beat the shit out of him and nearly killed him. Then, after he recovered, he went back to Vietnam and worked with the authorities until they'd found and arrested the jerks that jumped him. *That* . . . is badass. *That* should be a fucking movie, man. That guy . . . he can say whatever he wants about our videos. And he probably will.

One famous fan we are thrilled about is Chris McKay, who directed the *LEGO Batman* movie, a movie that you might recall opened with jokes about long opening logos and narration to start movies.

Twitter is this weird beast. It's like a digital front porch that allows anyone to come up to your front door and call you a piss-drinking whore. Famous people can be talked to . . . directly! And sometimes they talk back to you!

I try to remind myself that if I made a movie, it wouldn't be fun for people to make fun of it. I try to remind myself that we do have millions of fans that DO get the joke and ENJOY it. And that's more than we could have ever asked for.

We've made friends with Leonard Maltin and his daughter, Jessie. Leonard fucking Maltin. That was because of Kristian Harloff, who booked us on a movie trivia "Schmoedown" against the Maltins. (cough) We won (cough).

We've interacted online with Christopher McQuarrie, Scott Derrickson, Roger Corman, Michael Jai White, Andy Weir, and more. We even had Andy Weir on our podcast!

The fact that we've gotten those opportunities is absurd. There are movie-loving guys like us all over the planet. Many of them even make content; they just didn't happen to hit the right algorithm on the right day.

We try to be mindful of where we were when this all started, how far we've come, and how fortunate we are. We've had some strange and wonderful encounters.

When we first started out, we signed very early on with an MCN called The Collective. MCN stands for multi-channel network, and it's a company that has gone through YouTube certification, and they work with many channels to help them monetize videos and fight copyright claims. We signed with The Collective because that's where a few of our favorite creators were signed, but we've since moved to be represented by Made In Network in Nashville. They were forming and growing just as we were, and they've been an amazing help in growing our brand.

Anyway, back to The Collective. There was an Orlando convention for YouTubers, of which I forget the name . . . Prism or Sparkle or something. It ended up being almost exclusively preteen YouTubers and their fans—think *Hard Day's Night*, but with more glitter. But The Collective had a party one night for their creators. And I got to smoke a cigarette and talk with a dude from Corridor Digital, and then I peed next to either Rhett or Link—I'm just now realizing I've always seen them pictured together and I don't know which one is which. The non-glasses-wearing one. I peed next to him.

Then I drank seven Coronas and fell asleep on the bus back to the hotel. But that's another story for another time.

At a convention in Rhode Island, I ate lunch in the green room one table from Ron Perlman, then sat at our booth and watched Ralph Macchio sign autographs for over eight hours straight like some kind of absolute machine of kindness.

At a convention in Nashville we got to interview Jay Mewes and Brian O'Halloran, and then later we learned Kato Kaelin was MCing the main stage on the convention floor. So when we walked by, I yelled out "OJ did it!" Granted, I'd had some wine, but I probably would've done it sober too.

Fun fact: Chris and I have been in the same building as Kevin Smith—the man who first brought fame to us via Twitter—FOUR fucking times and have yet to meet him!

First, we went to see him in LA in 2015. Kevin was taping his podcast at a comedy club, and we got standby tickets and got in. We all had to sit separately from each other, but it was fun, though we didn't get to meet him.

Next, at C2E2 in Chicago, also in 2015, we were doing our panel the same time Kevin was doing his. Our panel had room for about seven hundred, and we were overwhelmed when over a thousand showed up and we had to turn people away. And when we left, we were a bit mobbed for autographs, which was, honestly, fucking awesome. It's anxiety-inducing, but awesome.

But we'd missed Kevin Smith again.

That night our Nashville Predators were in town to play the Chicago Blackhawks, and we decided to go. We lost the game and the series, and it sucked being there for that. But Kevin Smith had tweeted that *he* was at the game as well! Still didn't meet him.

A couple years later Smith came to Nashville and played the fucking Ryman—a big-deal old-school theater for *anyone* to play. We'd even emailed with him about meeting up backstage after, but then we encountered the most adamant rule-of-law-abiding-est teenage Ryman employee ever, and he was just not going to let us in.

"I don't suppose it would help if I showed you an email from Kevin Smith himself from two minutes ago telling me to come on back?" I asked.

"It won't," teen Robocop replied. Did not meet Kevin Smith again.

One other time later, when I was not present, Chris attended another Kevin Smith show and failed to meet him.

At this point it's like a game. How many times can we be in the same building and not meet him? Surely we're approaching *Guinness Book of World Records* status, no?

And if we ever did meet him, how could we ever repay him for his early support? How could we meet a former movie fan that turned himself into a moviemaker without throwing up a little on his hockey jersey? Maybe the universe is keeping us apart to help Chris and me avoid embarrassing ourselves.

CHAPTER 3

Bouncing the Juice
(AKA the Hustle)

When you find something that works, stick with it until it stops working. That was our early marketing philosophy for Cinema-Sins. But as a strategy for growth, it goes way back before us. "If it ain't broke, don't fix it" is a famous early variation of this phrase.

Growing up, I remember every now and then the political or economic climate would cause a certain sermon series Dad preached to have a bit more impact and echo among the congregation. Naturally, both he and the music director would try and recreate that kind of engagement by making a lot of the same choices or returning to the same scriptural bases for future services.

Sometimes a service would get emotional, and everyone would feel full of the Holy Spirit, and those services always seemed to get stretched on and on until the magic started to run out. I was in a five-hour revival service once, and I was a teenage believer at the time, and I remember thinking, "Does God care about our backs? Stomachs? Bladders?"

We heard sermons about single mothers. Sermons about drugs. Sermons about anything that was in the headlines. And it made sense. I never faulted my dad for preaching sermons that were partly related to current events. That's how you get people's attention.

If NASA had an event, sermons might focus on the bravery and courage of astronauts. During a presidential election, sermons would tend to encourage prayer and letting God lead your decisions in life. Even major sporting events got special sermons—I remember a prayer my father led the night of the Mike Tyson/Buster Douglas fight, and it was all about giving deference to God in everything, including housing situations *and* sporting events.

The philosophy is basically: do what's working as long as it works, and when it stops working just guess.

This is, believe it or not, how most American businesses and nonprofits and YouTube channels operate.

Like Comcast, which used to just provide cable TV packages. Then when the internet became a thing, they added that service. Today they offer cellular service, home phone service, and even home security services and products. Does it match their original core values? WHO CARES?! They just want money.

(Also, for the record, I personally doubt Comcast has ever had any core values.)

This is also true with film sequels. There's a reason we got half a dozen *Saw* movies, then after a short break, we're now getting another one. Bouncing the juice.

Remember in *Elf*, when the hired-gun children's book author says that they can't do fruits or vegetables because "everyone's doing small-town rural"? That's because everyone in that movie's publishing industry was . . . bouncing the juice.

Politics is all about taking what's working right now and riding it as long as possible before it gives out.

Music trends are this way. Remember when you first learned what ska was, and there were a dozen popular ska bands, and then three weeks later the entire genre was mostly dead?

The point is, most American kids grow up learning that time-tested phrase: if it ain't broke, don't fix it. And almost every operation that has made this their business plan has eventually seen it break and need fixing.

In theaters, we used to interlock films to bounce the juice. Again, this was back in the days of film. But if a movie suddenly started selling unexpectedly well or selling out shows on opening night, the home office would often ask us to take one of our prints and interlock it to a nearby auditorium.

Interlocking involves taking a single print of a movie—one film hard copy—and running it through two or more projectors at the same time. If it goes well, you double or triple your profits for a film. If it goes poorly, you give refunds or movie passes to a LOT more people. And interlocking is tricky. It's doable, even regularly, but it needs to be monitored five times more than a standard film projector situation, and it's prone to hiccups.

These days, with most theaters being digital now, it's just a matter of dropping a film into another auditorium's hard drive and selling tickets.

But in the days of film ... you had to run the film from the platter to and through the projector, then, at the bottom, instead of going back to the platters, you had to send that film to the next projector over through a series of floor and ceiling pullies.

Then you thread the second projector—leaving the right amount of slack between the two was crucial—and try and start both projectors at the same time. And now you're basically running one print through two projectors and doubling your money. And even though most box office money goes back to the studios for film rental costs, by adding another show, you let in another one hundred or more customers, many of whom bought concessions, which is where theaters make their money.

Oh, you want to know how theaters make their money? Well, that's a detour from the topic at hand, but I'm game if you are.

Theaters send back to studios over 90 percent of what they make at the box office. This is a rental fee. The longer a film stays in theaters, the lower the percentage of send-back money goes.

So this is why concessions are expensive as fuck and they don't let you bring in your own shit.

Do you have any idea how fucking cheap popcorn is? It's like ... cheap! But they sell a tub for $12, and we buy it because it's delicious and we're idiots.

Soft drinks are even less expensive for theaters. They actually get paid to sell the Coke or Pepsi products they sell. They make money twice every time you order a soft drink. And soft drinks cost a couple pennies for a large on the theater's end.

All the name-brand candies are marked up to hell and back, and even a bottle of Dasani water costs eight bucks. This is because the concessions are the only place theaters can really make money. And the money spent at concessions per all tickets sold, called the PerCap, is one of the most important numbers in all of movie theater management. All your payroll and inventory and cleaning costs can be through the roof, but if your PerCap is higher than average, you are Peyton Manning wrapped in a bear hug with Jesus himself . . . all being photographed by Annie Leibovitz.

So when you have a bad theater experience—maybe the floors are dirty or the cashier is distracted and bored, or if the picture is just a tiny bit blurry or the sound just a bit too quiet—try and remember that it's not *only* the theater's fault. The studios continue to force theater chains to take worse and worse deals, and that only causes cinemas to cut staff and lower standards.

Sometimes a movie makes a ton of money because of uniquely massive interest on the part of the public, regardless of the film's quality. Sometimes a film makes a ton of money because a core group of superfans keep going back to see it over and over.

But most of the time when a movie makes a lot of money, it's due to word of mouth: people seeing it, loving it, and telling their friends about it. *Shawshank Redemption* was one of these films for me in college. It was 1994, and I was fresh into my early college freedom of seeing movies.

But the small indie film *Shawshank Redemption* had yet to cross my path. I had heard of it, but the description sounded boring.

Ultimately enough friends that I trusted told me to go see it—word of mouth—that I went to see it. And of course I loved it, because it fucking rules. And maybe this is a bad example, because *Shawshank* didn't earn much at all at the box office and only climbed in acclaim and fan appreciation years later on home video. But it's still a movie I only saw because of word of mouth.

And to prove my point, plenty of films were word-of-mouth hits, like *The Hangover*; *Crouching Tiger, Hidden Dragon*; *Superbad*; and *Knives Out*. Word of mouth can kill a film or crown it, if the tide is strong enough.

And whether it's the water cooler at work, social networks, or any other form of communication, word of mouth still drives the bulk of what gets popular. Movies, music, even YouTube channels—if lots of people are talking about it, it's going to grow.

When that first Sins video ended up on the home page of Buzzfeed, it also ended up getting written about on a *Wired* blog. So I hit up that *Wired* author and offered an exclusive interview and prerelease of our next video. And it worked.

That next video, in part because of *Wired*'s coverage, got some viral action itself. This time it was "Everything Wrong With *The Avengers*." Of all the sites that wrote about the video, one that stuck out to me was *Forbes*. Fucking *Forbes*!

So I reached out to the *Forbes* author and did the same routine: "I'll give you an exclusive sneak peek at the next Sins video and an interview."

This became a pattern for the first several months of Cinema-Sins's existence. I strived quite hard to ensure beforehand some coverage for every new video release, and it worked for weeks. And at that point, I realized that our core audience was already there and committed, and I stopped caring as much about media coverage.

We had over 250,000 subscribers, and we were getting coverage on websites and blogs without even fishing for it anymore. So, around this time we started to experiment a bit.

Early on—like, first three weeks or so—I was convinced the format would need a shake-up after about six weeks. Maybe even "everything right with" for a bad movie, I'd suggested.

We were also fixated on keeping videos short. We thought for certain that longer videos would be a turnoff and we'd lose viewers and subscribers.

Quick aside: YouTube success, while awesome, brings its own set of unique problems and challenges. There's a reason why nearly every popular YouTuber I've ever met has anxiety or depression or both. The constant need to churn out regular content becomes a sort of digital twisted telltale heart, guilting you into pressing onward without break or vacation, constantly beating in your inner ear. Before you know it, your desire to keep riding the wave has left you exhausted, lonely, and creatively bored.

Only through experimentation and necessity did we end up testing the theory about the length of our videos, and boy were we wrong about needing to keep them short.

We tried to sin *The Room*, a notoriously bad movie, in late January of 2013. And we just couldn't find a way to actually include all the film's issues inside five minutes. So we just abandoned logic and released a video over eight minutes long—at the time an exceptionally long video compared to our channel average.

And you know what? People watched all 8.5 minutes. They loved it. They ate it up.

Just one year later we'd release our sins of *Batman & Robin*, which was a whopping twenty minutes long. And our viewers came with us, no matter the length. This was *way* before YouTube changed their approach and started valuing longer videos more, but we were fortunate to stumble early on a format that would later prove to be extra profitable.

The point is, we were liberated. For a long time we rushed the narration and overedited our scripts and videos in order to keep things under six minutes or so. Realizing fans were willing to watch to the end gave us time to breathe, let us explain certain sins more or with more words, and really got us humming on what has become our true video selves.

CHAPTER 4

Crossovers and Guests

Everyone needs a break. New voices can get your attention more. Being intentional about growth (spiritual or otherwise) is helpful to driving growth.

The Nazarene denomination's beliefs were mostly from the teachings of John Wesley. This meant that my father was definitely the "preacher" and was responsible for three sermons a week: Sunday morning, Sunday night, and Wednesday night.

But a pastor is more than a preacher. He or she is a shepherd, a counselor, a general manager, a makeshift therapist, an accountant, a janitor, and so much more. In many churches they do *everything*, from toilet cleaning to bill-paying to altar-prayer with members of the congregation. No matter what you believe regarding religion, it seems clear to me that most clergy are well-intentioned people with a work ethic that overshadows yours or mine.

These pastors are also often paid a shitty wage and asked to swallow it because housing is also provided for free, even though said housing is often awful or not up to standards. While the megachurches pay their pastors exorbitant riches in salary, most true pastors make a wage that puts them at or below the poverty line. Always on call, my father probably worked eighty hours a week my entire youth. I don't have to share his faith to be in awe of his work ethic.

A good pastor knows that every now and then, their preaching becomes too routine . . . too expected . . . too normal. This is the same reason hockey coaches mix up their line pairings or football teams fire the coach. New energy can spark growth.

That's why churches of almost all denominations have something called "revival," where a traveling preacher comes into town for one week's worth of special nightly services intended to fire up the peoples' souls and pocketbooks, and it almost always succeeds.

The traveling preacher was usually called an evangelist. Some were better than others, and as such, some cost more than others. But within the denomination, some can end up getting famous for their particular brand of preaching.

I remember a man named Stephen Manly. I saw him preach twice, once at an Indiana district-wide revival and once at a national gathering of Nazarenes. He had a unique ability to combine hand gestures with his words, and he repeated himself just enough that when he stopped using the words but only used the gestures, your brain knew what word he meant, and it made the moment all the more powerful for those in the audience.

Another traveling evangelist I recall had a voice that would echo like THUNDER through the church in a way that utterly demanded attention.

Sometimes Dad would swap pulpits with a nearby church—sometimes the same denomination and sometimes not—and he would go preach at their church, and they'd come preach at ours.

And sometimes, instead of guest preachers, Dad would invite a group of religious singers to spend the week ministering to our church in song. I greatly preferred the musical evangelists, because I had a love of music from an early age and by ten was already taking piano lessons. Music was more interesting to me than the message of the song, and for much of my youth that was as true of pop music as it was of church music.

The point is that even a faithful congregation can sometimes grow stagnant or stale, and a vibrant guest speaker or singer was a good way to kickstart things back into a livelier direction.

There's a reason this "mix it up" chapter comes AFTER the chapter about "bouncing the juice," because after the juice is gone and the bounce is done, you have to get creative and fresh to keep people's attention.

Another thing churches and religious organizations do a lot of is the retreat—everyone gets away to a lodge or cabin, team-building exercises occur, and everyone returns home rejuvenated in their faith.

I went to retreats as a middle schooler, a high schooler, a youth leader, a husband . . . believe me, churches have all kinds of retreats. Why? Because of the constant need to shake things up and keep the message fresh.

I remember one retreat when I was about sixteen, and in the first hour I began roughhousing with a friend and ended up with my head slammed into the corner of a coffee table. So while everyone else enjoyed the first night's worship service, I was at the hospital getting anesthetic shots in my fucking ear so they could sew it back together.

That retreat sucked, and we slept in a gymnasium in sleeping bags, but I do remember that the singer did a pretty good Phil Collins impression.

Companies have started doing retreats as well over the last few decades, taking the crew ziplining or rock climbing or camping. They call it "team building" today, but it's still just a corporate retreat—an attempt to get people out of their element and interacting together.

Just after I'd finally become a general manager of a movie theater after years as an assistant, I was invited to the corporate office's weeklong retreat and training program. It was free, and I took zero seconds to accept. I wanted to get better at my job so I could earn more money. If they were going to teach me, then I was going to learn.

The daytime portion of this company "retreat" was a classroom setting. I will admit that the sessions were led by a charming and hilarious corporate employee, and that made it easy for everyone to let our guards down and accidentally learn a few things.

In the evening, literally everyone went out to get drunk but me. I went out with everyone the first night, but it was disheartening to see how depressed everyone was and how much alcohol they were willing to throw at that condition. I didn't get drunk in those days, so I ordered takeout and went back to the hotel and watched TV. Smoked a little weed.

I feel like I missed out on a few things by not going out drinking, like camaraderie, community, and maybe even an STD or two. But I've always been glad I saved money and slept better than everyone else.

Over the course of the week, we took quizzes, got tips, had guest speakers, and did role-play scenes, and honestly most of us left with a genuine desire to be better at our jobs and improve our theater's operation.

I remember one fellow attendee (a theater manager) in my class was really mad that the company didn't test for marijuana. She brought it up several times, and no one had the heart to tell her that half the people in the training room, and indeed half the company, would be out of a job if we did drug testing.

Anyway, the training worked, for me at least. I realized I could earn more if my theater performed better overall, and I broke speed limits driving back home from Knoxville to Nashville, excited to implement new changes and have a staff meeting.

I personally came home fired up and immediately implemented tons of ideas I'd learned, like employee incentive promotions, group sales techniques, and much more.

The retreat/training had done its job, and I was lit with a new fire for success. This is the reason companies have retreats. Or group conferences. Everyone needs to get fired up now and again. Everyone gets bogged down in the details of a job.

One of the lessons we learned in this weeklong training was about employee property. Specifically, we were not allowed, as managers, to search an employee's purse or backpack. The rule seemed harmless at the time, but in just a few weeks I came face to face with an example.

The most ridiculous call I ever got as a floor manager was regarding a money clip. A gentleman had come to see a nine o'clock show and had realized in the parking lot afterwards that he was missing his money clip.

He didn't say "money clip" though, he said, "money clip with ten thousand dollars cash."

Now look, I could probably write an entire book about the kind of dumbass that walks around with ten thousand dollars cash in a money clip in his pocket. I'm tempted to. Because that is a giant dumbass of a human being.

But as manager, it's my job to try and help the dumbass customer retrieve their lost property.

So … first things first, we go to the theater he saw the movie in and turn on the bright overhead cleaning lights, and he searches the area where he was sitting.

He finds nothing.

Now, my ushers at the time were excellent cleaners. They didn't miss anything. Why? Because they were good workers. But also because they were all hoping to be the one to find whatever change or bills fell out of someone's pocket during that show. And you can't check thoroughly for quarters without basically sweeping thoroughly.

On the way back up front to customer service the dude is in a panic. He's certain some other customer or one of our ushers found his money clip and stole it.

As fate would have it, we pass all three of my closing ushers in the hallway. They've all clocked out and are headed home.

I stop them and ask if anyone saw any money clip or anything like it.

And one kid goes white as a ghost. Let's call him Spencer.

And Spencer begins to sweat.

"No," he says.

"Nope," responds Eric.

"No," Tony declares.

But everyone is focused on Spencer and his obviously lying ass. This motherfucker, I am certain, has the money clip and the $10K in his backpack right fucking now!

I have just returned from corporate training. And I know that I cannot search an employee's bag without permission.

There's nothing I can do but let them all go.

Rich bitch dude barks at me all the way back up to customer service, saying I'd let the guilty kid go, which I had. But I can't tell you how little sympathy I had for this fool.

And I don't believe for a second he had ten grand in cash on a money clip. I've seen too many liars and exaggerators. He had lost maybe a thousand bucks, tops.

Imagine ten grand in a money clip. It literally has to be all thousand-dollar-bills, or else no money clip could hold that amount. And you don't just happen upon thousand-dollar bills! You don't go to an ATM and withdraw a thousand bucks and get a single bill!

So, say this guy's ten grand would more likely have been in hundreds. That's a hundred hundreds. In a single money clip. Which is laughable.

So in a way, everyone sucks in this story, except for me. I followed the rules and ended up getting to make fun of both the thief and the victim.

For a while, CinemaSins employed the same "guest speaker" logic of my religious upbringing. Bring in a new voice to shake things up and get the juices flowing. But we have had middling success with this tactic at best.

Over the years we've had a handful of guest narrators. Most have been soundly rejected by our fans.

Only Neil deGrasse Tyson was able to help us narrate without catching too much hell. He helped us sin a few science fiction films, and we were never more honored.

But we also had Kevin Smith, Game Theory and Movie Theory, Matthew Santoro, and Doug from Channel Awesome as guest narrators—hell, Doug even helped us write the script for the sins of the live-action *Grinch* movie to make sure they all rhymed like Dr. Seuss himself had written them!

We were honored each time. But our fans have not historically been very kind to the various guest narrators we've had over the years, which unfortunately scared off a few cool guest narrators we were working on locking in.

Kevin Smith even apologized in the comments for "ruining" the Sins experience for anyone by guest-narrating, since he was a fan himself. And for the record, he didn't ruin shit. The pouty little entitled fans that dragged his narration appearance ruined things. By being dicks.

Whatever. I'm a Kevin Smith fan to the grave, and y'all else can just take a walk. Kevin Smith went from movie fan to moviemaker, and almost *none* of us self-proclaimed cinephiles can or ever will be able to claim that.

We had plans for him to do *Empire* and *Jedi*, but he was

adamant about not changing the experience for fans. Because Kevin Smith is more of a CinemaSins fan than the CinemaSins fans that were bitching about Kevin Smith as a guest narrator.

Of course, he's the dude who tweeted to help make us popular, and one of our heroes was just getting unfairly dunked on by entitled fans. That fucking rocked me, man. For real. That was Thanksgiving Day. I remember because I was with my extended family, and I was pouting all day and everyone kept asking me why. And I didn't want to let my first-world problems ruin Thanksgiving.

We haven't had a guest narrator since then. And we probably won't. We are obviously growing and adding new channels and will introduce some new narrators soon, but we're done with the crossover episodes and stunt narrators. Our fans don't want them, and we don't want the grief from fans about it.

But we had a few lined up that would have been so sweet. All of our guest narrators were awesome, but we had some bigger ones planned before the audience basically made it known they wanted *nothing* to do with guest narrators.

And that made my life fun. If there's one aspect of my job that gets old quick, it's narrating. I am so fucking tired of narrating. I wish someone would come along with a pitch-perfect imitation of my Sin voice, and I'd pay them whatever it took for me to take a year off from narration without the fans rioting. God, that is literally a description of Heaven right there.

Love you, Sins fans, more than humbled at our success, but I'm so fucking tired of narrating I could eat a wildebeest.

The original plan actually was for Chris and I to alternate narrations. But just when we launched, he had a family tragedy and was out of pocket for a couple weeks. So I did the first three narrations.

By the time Chris was back and ready to go with our sins video for *Prometheus*, the fans seemed to have already made up their minds about the Sins voice . . . with many of the comments asking why there was a new narrator.

So, quite by accident, I became the "voice of CinemaSins." The only voice. At least until the podcast.

But when people get nasty online about our videos, they don't reference the entire team or the company name, they reference me, Jeremy. And if you see that enough over time, it begins to make you feel like shit, no matter how good your mental health is.

CHAPTER 5

Growing a Business and Hiring Friends

When I was growing up, I had a bunch of friends, but none of them were really lifelong or anything.

We moved about every five or six years, because that's normal for preachers and their families in many denominations. And so my first five and a half years were spent living in Baltimore, Maryland. This gave me a love of the Orioles and a good friend named . . . shit, what was her name? Patty? Lucy? Pam?

The next five years, basically all of elementary school, were spent in Angola, Indiana, a town up in the tight northeast corner of Indiana, just miles from the Michigan border. No lie, having been to Michigan was worth a great deal of social street cred in elementary school.

Here I walked to school twelve blocks, by myself. It was the '80s, so we just trusted everyone not to be kidnapping assholes.

My best friends there were Ben and John. Hey, what do you know? I remembered their names!

Ben had more Transformers than me and a backyard with a woods and a creek . . . while John lived on a farm and had lots of animals.

Oh, and Tracy—the tomboy girl on my baseball team!

These were good years.

This town had one movie theater with one auditorium—it ran *E.T.* for more than a year straight! This is the theater where I saw *The Care Bears Movie* and *The Black Cauldron*.

After fifth grade we said goodbye to another set of friends and moved to the tiniest town to ever exist anywhere on the planet: Ossian, Indiana. Here, my best friends were Andy and Vince, my two neighbors. I also made friends with baseball and educational mates Jason, Jason, Sean, Mickey, and Mike. (The further we get into my story the more of my friends' names I remember, which makes sense).

We lived here for another five years and then moved again, further south in the state, to Anderson, Indiana. It was between my sophomore and junior years of high school, which is a shitty time to have to move for a teenager.

My best friend here was definitely Andy—different Andy. We shared a sense of humor, love of music, and similarly strict parents. I miss him.

In my first eighteen years of life, I was never in a position to hire a friend, but I certainly played on baseball teams, joined clubs, participated in academic bowl, played basketball, and spent a lot of team time with them. And every team I ever shared with a friend was better for it.

I managed movie theaters for about ten years, most of them as an assistant or first assistant manager. Eventually I did get a theater of my own to run, a ten-screen in the suburbs.

Boy, did I luck out. The staff was not only full of hardworking kids, they were like a family. I was coming from a twenty-seven-screen theater where we had to hire five new people every goddamn week. Here at the ten-screen, everyone did their jobs and did so with a smile, and I rode that shit for two full years.

If any new applicants were friends with one or more employees . . . I saw that as a bonus and hired them. Only a few times did that strategy ever burn me. Most of the kids in this town were just honest, hardworking teenagers. I was only seventeen miles from my previous theater, where basically a teen that worked hard was an anomaly. The employees here, on the other hand, were so good they even accidentally won a combo contest.

See, corporate likes to push the combos, because that is the way they get the most of your money. So every quarter there's a combo-selling contest among the entire company—with theaters being placed in "flights" based on similar attendance and box office numbers.

So one quarter, my crew of badasses sold so many combos our theater placed in the combo-selling contest. What did we win?

Not much. Not "we" anyway. I, personally, as the general manager, won a trip for two to a cattle-drive weekend in Dallas, Texas. The teenage employees who'd actually sold all the combos? They got nothing. And that's basically everything you need to know about corporate America right there in one little story.

Anyway, I was not allowed to let any of the employees go on the trip, so of course I went on the cattle-drive trip, because, "Hey, free trip."

I asked my roommate at the time, Josh, if he wanted to go with me, and he was like, "Hey, free trip."

Because corporations rarely plan ahead, our cattle drive in Dallas—actually Fort Worth, but don't get me started on *that* whole thing—took place in July. Yes, let's go to Texas in the hottest month of the year. Sounds fun. I remember getting off the plane and finally walking out of the airport into the Dallas air and feeling like I was breathing in burning sand. "Fuck Dallas" became a bit of a running joke that weekend for Josh and me.

We got there a few hours early, so we went and found a pizza shop and ate some food. Then we met up at the meet-up time with all the other theater managers who'd won the combo contest (and their guests) as well as most of the corporate office staff. The corporate office people, you see, they got to go on *all* the trips. Theater managers had to either bust ass to motivate the staff to sell combos or luck out like I did, but the executives just got a free trip every quarter. Like assholes. Again . . . welcome to American capitalism, where the workers eat shit while the bosses get perks and raises and eventually golden parachute severance packages when they are accused of sexual harassment.

Anyway, we showed up for the meet-up and the first scheduled event was a trip to a famous BBQ joint for dinner—even though we'd just eaten pizza an hour earlier. Thanks for telling me ahead of time, jerks. How hard is it to send an itinerary *before* the trip?

This place was nuts too. Line dancing, BBQ (good food), and a fucking bull-riding cow-roping ring RIGHT INSIDE THE RESTAURANT! Crazy.

Since we'd already eaten, Josh and I had some beers and goofed off in the gift shop. When the buses dropped us all off at the hotel in Fort Worth, they said we had to be ready to leave the next morning at 4:00 a.m. They weren't joking, and I was pissed.

Getting up at four in the morning is something everyone should do at least once, right? A lot of the cattle-drive trip was going to be new for me: being in Texas, riding a horse, firing a gun, pretending to like my coworkers and bosses.

We all zombie-shuffled out to the bus at 4:00 a.m., and half of us slept the entire way out to the ranch, which meant we got a second rude awakening from Mrs. Screamy McStereotype Ranch Owner. She was a drill sergeant, and we all filed in and followed her instructions, if only because we were too fucking tired to object or ask questions.

Turns out the first order of business was something called a Cowboy Breakfast, and honestly it sounded fucking righteous. I didn't care if cowboys ate cow testicles for breakfast, I was going to chow the fuck down.

But first we had to ride out there. So they piled us all on two trailers with hay bales . . . and the hired cowboys on their horses and mules kept pace with the tractors pulling us. One of them was on a donkey, or a mule. Or a burro. Josh and I weren't sure.

But we quickly became more concerned with which of us could pull off the most authentic Spanish-sounding accent while saying the word "burro."

"Burro," I offered, rolling my R's a bit.

"Buhroh," Josh responded, rolling the R's but adding a softening H quality.

"Boohroh," I tried, with a little too much O sound.

"Burhreau?" Josh asked.

We traded attempts at least three more times, each more comically over-pronounced (and probably borderline racist) than the one before.

Next to us sat the head of concessions for the entire company. He was not only not entertained by our dialogue, he was also still half asleep and grumpy. Without hesitation he declared, "You two are idiots." Then he turned to face out the other side of the trailer.

Josh and I just laughed, because we already knew we were idiots, and we were kind of impressed it had only taken this long to let the company executives on the trip know that as well.

We spent the rest of the ride giggling and wondering why the hell they had to build the breakfast campfire forty minutes away from the main ranch area. Soon enough, we didn't care.

Turns out a "cowboy breakfast" is really just cooking everything together in one giant-ass skillet. I'm talking about a skillet five feet in diameter. This skillet could double as a dinner table under the right circumstances.

Eggs, bacon, potatoes, sausage, and even the coffee ... all cooked in the same massive cast-iron frying pan.

And it all tasted amazing. Though I wonder if the taste was directly related to them having made us wake up at 4:00 a.m. and then ride a bus for two hours and *then* ride a trailer for forty minutes. Would literally anything edible have tasted amazing in that moment? I bet it would have.

Then, after the cowboy breakfast, they drove us to Murder Grove, AKA the six-shooter shooting gallery. Because this cattle-drive cowboy experience comes complete with the chance to literally fire a gun.

They set us up in a basic opening between groves of trees. Fifteen feet away was a series of hay bales with bottles on top of them. Everyone was going to get a chance to fire six shots from an old cowboy gun, and whoever hit the most bottles won, well, something—I forget what, probably a confederate flag decal or some shit.

I moved to the back of the group instinctively. I'd never fired a gun. I'd never held a gun. I didn't want to, if I'm honest.

I just kept thinking, as theater managers and corporate jerks took turns firing six shots each, "Any one of these fools could turn around and shoot me in the face if they wanted, and there are *zero* checks and balances in place to stop it." And I was right. Any one of those fools could have killed me. When it was my turn, I thought briefly of trying to make a point with my shots but decided against it and fired all six rapidly into the hay bale backstops then dropped the gun in the instructor's hands as soon as it was empty.

Look, plenty of people I respect and love own guns and use them for hunting or self-defense or for target shooting. And I'm not trying to hate on guns. But for me, growing up a preacher's kid, sheltered from even movie violence let alone real violence, holding a gun felt dangerous, sinful, and wrong. It frightened me beyond expectation.

Make of that what you will.

Also, when I told Josh I was writing a chapter for my book

about our cattle-drive trip, the first word out of his mouth was "Burro!"

———•———

The next phase of the cowboy experience was the titular cattle drive. But first they had to teach us all how to ride a horse.

This is where they make their money.

Some of us learned faster than others. Like Josh and me, who bonded to our horses pretty quickly and then had to wait around an hour while all the idiot losers took their sweet time getting comfortable with a horse.

My horse didn't turn left for me when I asked him to, though he turned right with no issue. I named him Zoolander.

Now let's be real about this event. These cattle we were driving were miniature cows. Not baby cows. Just tiny cows, bred to be cute. They'd run this route we were leading them on hundreds of times, and they probably didn't need much cowboy guidance to make the trip. This was more about letting guests "feel" like they "drove the cattle" than any actual cattle-driving skill-transferring kind of training. But still, we all signed a waiver about random horse death, and then we all had to learn to ride a horse. Then, finally, we got to "drive" the cattle about a mile or so. Maybe two.

Let me ask you this: what do you think happens when a bunch of general managers used to calling all the shots get lumped together and asked to collectively herd cattle in a certain direction and work as a team?

The answer is: thirty or forty bossy voices yelling out commands that none of the other bossy people are following. Absolute chaos.

After about five minutes, most of the group ambled to the back of the pack, where they gossiped about theater stuff while telling themselves they were "driving" the cattle forward.

Meanwhile, the three professional cowboys that worked for this ranch, along with me and Josh, did the real work of driving the cattle. The five of us stayed in front of and beside the group of cows, checking the strays and setting the pace.

It was actually pretty fucking fun. It was not unlike a video game, in that every few minutes one cow would break off, and I'd go chasing him down, only to have two more wander off while I was redirecting the first. But I'd still somehow manage to corral all three back to the herd without losing too much ground or time.

You might think I'm joking about how all the other theater worker attendees hung back in a huge group while we did all the work, but let's just say that Josh and I were sitting down inside the air-conditioned lunch barn with full plates when the first of the stragglers walked in. And by that time we'd also already been offered jobs as show cowboys by the woman who owned the ranch—that's how good we'd been at handling the horses and directing the cattle! Mrs. Screamy McStereotype loved us!

And for a few moments, we considered it. That's how terrible it is to manage a movie theater for a living.

When we got back to our hotel rooms that afternoon, about 4:00 p.m., there were custom embroidered blue-jean jackets with the company logo on the back laid out on each bed.

And my first thought was actually, "They came in our room

when we weren't here?!" Because, seriously, what the fuck? Even to do a surprise gift thing, that's creepy and unlawful as hell!

But also … a jean jacket? A jean jacket?! This was 2002, so long after jean jackets had faded from popularity and long before they'd made a retro-fashionable return, thereby demonstrating the corporation's finger-on-pulse understanding of their employees or even the lives of normal people.

That night there was a banquet, and an hour beforehand, in the lobby, my district manager caught up to me and Josh and seemed frantic. "You're not wearing jeans to the banquet, are you? You can't wear jeans. The CEO hates jeans, and he has been known to call people out that dress too casually for the banquet! The company spent a lot of money on this trip, you know."

I think he said some other weasel words and phrases, but the point had been received.

And as much as I hated caving to "the man," I didn't want to be the only asshole getting singled out by the CEO for wearing jeans to an awards banquet.

Josh and I hopped in a cab, and I said, "The Gap. The nearest Gap."

The nearest Gap store was seven miles outside the city, and it took us nearly twenty minutes to get there.

And there in that Gap store in Eastern Fort Worth, Texas, occurred the fastest retail transaction of all time. As I entered, I spied a table of khaki pants between myself and the cashier. I grabbed three pair as I passed, and quickly scanned them for sizes as I walked. I found a 34/34, which would do fine—I was more of a 33/32, but times were tight—and I dropped the other two pairs as I reached the checkout.

I slapped the pants down, swiped my card, and we were out of there inside of a minute.

I changed in the cab, and we arrived back at the hotel four minutes before the banquet, which we ran to and ended up hot and sweaty for.

Oh, and 30 percent of the attendees in the room were wearing FUCKING BLUE JEANS!

I shot fire eyes at my district manager as he pretended to enjoy his baked potato.

You know what they didn't do on this trip? They never took us to a movie. They never even took us to a local theater we could tour. And this was the moment I realized that theater companies didn't want film fans as managers and projectionists . . . they wanted sheep. They wanted cheap idiots and bean counters. But they didn't want passionate movie lovers.

And that realization made me sadder than it probably should have. But that trip—specifically the return flight home—is when I began to think about leaving the movie theater business once and for all.

And ten months later, I did.

Most people who work at a job wish their job was better. Some hate it; some merely wish for changes. And I realize that I'm beyond lucky to be able to "work" by making videos on YouTube.

But it affords me the chance to work with people I know and trust. Not people who will call me an idiot for over-pronouncing "burro." Not people that hate having to have a job.

But my friends. People who care about me, and by extension care about my brand and its survival.

I remember early in CinemaSins's run, I was still doing regular online video reviews of movies and shows with my buddy Aaron Dicer. We'd gone to college together, and he had his own pop-culture podcast where he reviewed content with guests.

And one day I mentioned "those videos that count all of a movie's sins," and Aaron said he'd seen those videos.

I waited a beat. "No, that's me. That's me narrating those. I'm making those videos."

His mind was briefly blown, and I teased him about not recognizing my voice.

A couple years later he wrote some sins for *La La Land* on a lark and sent them to me. And they were good. So I put them into my own script for that movie and didn't tell Chris about it.

And it was only a few months later we started talking about a real job opportunity. Then Aaron went full-time with us, and our writing has been better ever since.

Listen, some people will tell you *not* to hire your friends. Don't mix business and pleasure. You've heard this, right?

Well, if you adhere to that, then you have shitty friends.

If you have good friends, then they share your moral fiber, work ethic, and loyalty.

CinemaSins's entire staff has been built on a "hire your friends" philosophy.

Our first full-time hire was Barrett Share, our friend. He had nagged us about starting a podcast and had been contract writing for us on the Music Video Sins channel.

When he moved back to Nashville, we hired him full-time to write sins, edit videos, and manage the podcast.

After Barrett, our next hires were Aaron and Jonathan. Aaron was my friend from college, but he had guested on the CinemaSins *SinCast* podcast and knew the other guys. Jonathan had been friends with Barrett and Chris for years and knew movies like an encyclopedia—especially horror films.

The only other hire since has been Deneé, who was already a longtime friend of Aaron's but who had met the sin gang a couple of times.

Hiring friends is only bad business strategy when you have awful friends. Otherwise, it's an *excellent* business strategy!

Allow me to explain further: hiring your friends only gets tricky when you have to discipline them for poor work. But if they are good friends, they aren't going to slack off or do bad work. In fact, a friend is much more likely to actually give a shit whether your business succeeds or fails *because* they are your friend.

In addition, you should know your friends pretty well in terms of their strengths and weaknesses, and therefore, you're better able to place them in a role in which you know they can succeed.

CHAPTER 6

All the Shit We Tried
that People Hated

Being a senior pastor is hard, man. If you're the leader of a church, you are never off duty. You wear lots of badges and do lots of jobs. But you are ultimately judged by the church board, and the greater governing body, mostly on your membership growth and your finances.

Yes, kids, a church is judged by its superiors like any other business. Shocker.

If you don't increase the attendance and/or the revenue after a few years, you are not going to stay there long. So pastors get creative. They try new ideas.

After a surprisingly well-attended youth event, my father decided to add a youth band to morning worship, including electric guitars and drums and keyboards AND brass instruments!

And he got kickback for that.

Granted, this was the '90s, but to have members of the church tell you that electric guitars are evil, even while the kids playing the instruments were only there because of this band . . . well, it's disheartening.

And honestly, he got kickback on any new idea, simply because it was a new idea.

We tried puppets, but no one ever came to practice.

Teen Bible Quizzing proved popular with . . . three teens, two of which were my brother and I, and we were there by coercion.

I remember an outdoor tent service that had twice as many bee attendees as it did humans.

Any youth event that had music would cause at least one board member to grouse about dancing. And yet these board members were all just fine with us calling Sunday night after-church events "afterglows" because they either trusted we teens were clueless to the word's meaning or because they didn't care. Or *they* didn't know the word's original meaning.

Point is, the teens knew.

Singspirations! That was another of my dad's ideas that I loved. Sunday evening services that had no sermon, just all songs and singing! Honestly, even when I was a believer, the music was always the best thing about being a Christian. So an entire service of music and no boring sermon? Sign me UP!

People didn't exactly love it. Why? Because people are cranks, and if you go to a church long enough, you start to feel like you own part of it and then you start acting like a dickhead. It did last several years, though, so I suppose it was one of the better "new ideas" the church had seen in a while.

This was a church where every Sunday morning service you could hear the blatant sound of some old lady in the back clipping her fingernails during the sermon, by the way. Sigh.

Try as he might, my dad couldn't seem to grow the congregation size. Because that wasn't his job. Dad was a healing pastor. He came in after a church split and worked for a few years to heal the rift and pain, and then he'd move on and let another growth-oriented pastor take over. I used to mock him for all the churches he left *right before* they got popular. Because I was a clueless little shit.

So I saw my father's attempts to bring in new people to the church as failed, but he saw them as above and beyond the requirements of his job. He was here to heal hearts, friendships, families. Any growth while he was here was icing on the cake.

And yet he still tried. He tried so hard everywhere we went. He tried to grow every congregation he ever led. Not because he was stubborn, but because he wanted to please God. He wanted to do his spiritual job and *then* do more. Just like Jesus did. No matter where I settle on the believer/nonbeliever spectrum, I will always respect my father's commitment.

The second theater chain I worked for had a training program for managers that they were very proud of. Some of it was useful. It was a week of school at the home office where everyone went out drinking every night and the biggest takeaway for most people was the movie theater version of Shrute Bucks—a way for you to bribe employees to earn points for good behavior and work to gain rewards.

I actually had a bigger takeaway. They told a story about taking a problem customer, someone who complains all the time, and turning them into a fan by making them feel important. You make them a secret shopper. "Hey," you say, "You are really good at spotting where we are falling short. Would you mind being my personal secret shopper whenever you come in? Just take notes, and when your movie is over, give the notes to me so I can improve our operation. Would you be interested in that?"

This blew my mind. I love reverse psychology. I love disarming people that are angry by being kind instead. The whole thing appealed to me.

And wouldn't you know, about four months later, I had my first repeat complainer. "The floors are dirty," he said. Or the sound was too quiet, or the bathrooms smelled bad. By the third complaint I recognized the guy and his wife, and I went right for the jugular with the freshly learned technique.

I gave him the spiel about being a secret shopper, and he fucking fell for it completely. He was nearly salivating by the end of it. "I'll even give you some movie passes so you can come more often without paying more out of pocket," I added for good measure.

And I'll be damned if it didn't do wonders. The next time I saw him, he was smiling ear to ear, and he had a clipboard. He'd made a chart himself, printed it out, and brought it on the clipboard.

"You won't be a very secret 'secret shopper' if you're walking around taking notes on a clipboard," I informed him. He agreed. I traded him a pad of sticky notes for the clipboard.

He saw his movie, he came by on his way out to give me his notes, and he was still grinning ear to ear. By making him part of the team, we'd taken away the edge of his anger.

So this went on for a couple months. He would come in every weekend with his wife. The routine was always the same. And sure, I had to take time out myself to talk to him every time, but at least he wasn't complaining anymore. I had turned my complainer into a happy assistant.

One afternoon he came out of a movie, chatted me up a moment, and headed outside to his car. Now, for this theater in particular—every theater is different—we had paid security guards on duty pretty much anytime we were open. They were all local PD or county sheriff's officers. That day's officer walked up to me, pointing at my secret shopper as he left, and asked what the story was.

So I gave him the elevator-pitch version of learning the technique at the home office and using it on this guy.

And the officer grimaced. "I arrested that guy," he said.

"For what?" I was shocked, but not as much as I was about to be.

"Child pornography," he replied. "Guy and his wife took sick pictures of their own kids."

And I had him scrutinizing and interacting with my high school employees. My stomach sank. What had I done?

The next time he came in, I planned to tell him that corporate was cracking down on theaters having their own secret shoppers, and we had to stop doing it. But I never saw him again. I figure he probably recognized one of the police officers that had arrested him and found a new theater to watch movies in.

My point is that even really good ideas—ones that have been proven to work before—aren't always the right solution. Nothing works out quite like you planned it.

———◆———

Back when I was worried, early on, about keeping things fresh at CinemaSins, it was probably just Chris and I feeling like things were too good to be true. Feeling like we didn't deserve the success we were having. Worried about how to keep it up.

We tried a variety of secondary video content, and none of it ever really caught on with the fans, though each now-defunct series still has its devotees.

I stared a series called "Conversations With Myself About Movies," where I used split-screen editing to have debates about movies with two extreme ends of my own personality. These were incredibly fun to make, but they took a lot of time, mostly in the memorization of the script. I had to memorize each half of each script and learn it well enough to know all the beats and pauses in order to play "both" roles.

I started doing a cooking show called "Movie Recipes" in my kitchen, where recipes were based on movies but were intentionally designed to sound and taste like shit. Every episode ended with me vomiting in the sink. It was fun and sort of charming, I thought, in a garage-band kind of way. But it never took off.

Years later we'd revive the "Movie Recipes" series, only this time going fine dining, working with top-tier chefs tasked with cooking a meal inspired by a favorite movie. We went to DC, did some in Nashville, went to Atlanta, and ate an absolute fuckton of amazing food.

But again, the series never found much of an audience. I suspect to this day that the show was great, but the CinemaSins YouTube channel wasn't the right outlet for it. The show remains in my pocket for a future relaunch.

We recorded a fucking theme song, in a real recording studio. And no, you can't hear it. Because it didn't turn out like we wanted. We spent a couple days writing lyrics and then speak-singing in a recording studio, and at the time we thought we were making some excellent shit. But there's a reason you've never heard that song.

For a while we worked with a couple writers who wanted to help us do the sins of the Harry Potter books. Weeks were spent on research and writing, only for all of us to eventually realize: there's no way to visually represent a book's contents in a YouTube video.

BrandSins is another whole story. We started the channel with the best of intentions, with a new host and new format, and no one liked it. So we switched it up, making it a bit more like the main CinemaSins videos, but it got no traction. We eventually signed over ownership of the channel to another entity and haven't been involved with it since. It'd be awesome if you stopped asking me about it on Twitter. 'Kay, thanks.

We set up a hotline. An honest-to-goodness hotline, where people could call and leave us messages. The idea was for them to narrate their own sins. But we got all *kinds* of weird shit.

We made one video using some of the messages, and the person who left the messages asked us to delete the video because he was embarrassed. And even though we had a legal disclaimer, we killed the video. We don't want to insult fans or make them targets.

Since then, the hotline has remained open. It still gets calls to this day. But we haven't done anything with any of the messages, mostly because we're all so busy we keep forgetting about it altogether. And the messages continue to be pretty nutty.

Perhaps our most hated "new thing" was when we swapped concepts with Honest Trailers for *The Amazing Spider-Man 2*. Which makes me sad to this day, because we had some great jokes in there. But we ultimately tinkered with the audio effects too much and made the "trailer voice" so robotic people couldn't focus on anything else.

We have also definitely swung and missed on a number of merchandising ideas, including designs as well as partnerships.

One of the things we vowed never to do was to endorse some shitty product we didn't actually try and didn't actually believe in.

Our advertisers to date all meet that criteria: NatureBox, Harry's, MUBI, BetterHelp, Likewise ... even advertisers we were unable to check out personally we have vetted extensively. We don't want to take ad dollars directly from a company whose product or values directly contradict our own. We don't want to take money to tell you to buy crappy products. This is partly because we're decent people, but also partly because if you send your fans to enough shady vendors, they will stop trusting you and eventually stop even listening to you completely.

We've left a lot of money on the table here. And I'm not

bragging. Well, I am bragging about our collective moral integrity. But I bet you've heard podcasts where they rattle off a dozen sponsors before they get started, and I'm really fucking glad we've never become that.

CHAPTER 7

The Movies that Hooked Me

Because I was largely forbidden from going to the cinema as a child, a lot of the attachments I formed to films occurred during a sheltered upbringing. For instance, *Candleshoe* and *The Muppets Take Manhattan* were two of my very favorite films growing up, because they were both full of adventure, laughs, and clean content my parents approved of. I've watched both again now as an adult, and they hold up well. It makes me smile to know that even sheltered-me had pretty good taste. But as a kid, I thought everyone watched *Candleshoe* every other day.

I was, of course, quite taken with *Star Wars* and *Back to the Future* and the like, along with my peers, except I came to all those movies two years late, whenever they were available for borrowing from the library. Rarely did we rent a movie from a video store, and if we did it would be something like *Jesus of Nazareth* or *Amazing Grace and Chuck*.

I was so surrounded by wholesome shit that the first time I

saw porn I threw up. And some of you might think that is the conservative upbringing doing its job, but I say ... throwing up sucks, and porn—or at least sex—is inevitable, so it seems cruel to me not to be more open with our American kids about our bodies and sex.

My mother was pretty obsessed from childhood with *White Christmas* and also *Star Trek*. So I was raised with a heavy dose of both. *Brady Bunch* reruns were fine. The old Adam West *Batman* episodes were fine. *Happy Days*, *Family Ties*, and *The Cosby Show* were all fine. It's not as though I had zero connection to mainstream entertainment. It's just that I was so sheltered from the other stuff that when I saw it, I was shocked. That goes for the violence of *Predator* and the blatant sexuality of *Basic Instinct*.

I remember being at a sleepover with other Christian kids where we watched *Indiana Jones and the Last Crusade*. It was my first Indiana Jones movie, and I loved it. I was a young teenager.

My parents were pissed that I had been shown this movie, and they let it be known.

Imagine being the kid whose parents call the sleepover parent to complain about a harmless movie being too violent. How many of those kids at the party do you think ever invited me to anything again? The answer is zero.

For the record, I don't blame my folks here. I think a lot of parents try to keep their kids from seeing too much violence or sexuality in media, and even a PG-13 film these days can be pretty racy.

But the more I was kept from seeing movies, the more I wanted to see movies. It was the Streisand effect, years before the internet existed and the Streisand effect would be named.

My older brother was really my gateway to movies. He would come home from college and tell me about films he'd seen. When I was a high school sophomore and he was a college freshman, he came home for Christmas break and snuck me off with him to see *JFK*, a movie that left both of us stunned. This was pre-internet, as my CinemaSins business partner, Chris Atkinson, says, so it was easy to believe a lot of the movie's claims without the ability to instantly fact-check things.

That same break, our parents had a weekend marriage retreat, so it was just my brother and me. And he rented *T2: Judgment Day*, which he had seen in theaters but which had come out on VHS in November. He gave me five minutes of explanation of the first movie as background knowledge—since I had never seen the first Terminator film—then he showed me *T2*, and my mind exploded completely.

That is the movie that hooked me on movies forever, and it's all because my brother showed it to me. He was my dealer into the drug world of film. Next came *Jurassic Park*, then *Pulp Fiction*, *Apollo 13*, and *Twister* locked me in on a very serious level. If movies were heroin, I'd have been shooting up constantly. I couldn't get enough movies.

Just going to see *Jurassic Park* in 1993 was a highlight of my movie-loving life. I stayed up all night to finish reading the book. I finished reading around ten in the morning and slept for six hours before heading to the theater.

And yes, the movie changed a lot of the book (just let Hammond be evil!), but the movie is still a moviegoing highlight for me. Incredible practical effects (RIP Stan Winston), tight story, typical Spielberg tension. I don't remember a lot of my theater experiences, but this one is top five for sure.

———●———

When you start working at a movie theater, a lot of the magic of the environment dissipates. Having your home or apartment smell like popcorn sucks. Having to be polite to racists and drunks and other assholes sucks. Sweeping up trash all the time is awful, and apologizing to assholes while giving them movie passes eventually starts to gnaw at your soul.

People are terrible. They're messy, selfish, and rude, and theater workers get paid very little money to deal with these animals. And clean up after them—what is it about a movie theater that makes people just leave garbage everywhere? They don't do this at the grocery store!

My favorite part of theater management was booth work, where I got to build movies from reel to print and ensure overall quality of presentation. That was when I felt most connected to the "magic" of movies and the cinema experience.

I probably sold a thousand hot dogs or more while working for theaters, but there's no magic in that, trust me. The magic is in the experience, which is mostly controlled by your friendly neighborhood projectionist. Picture quality, sound quality, lights: all controlled from the booth. Not to mention the build of the film itself.

Movies, back in my day, in the '90s, arrived to theaters in metal canisters, in separate twenty-minute reels. And it was our job to take those separate reels, usually six or seven, and combine them into one long "reel" we could put on a platter and show to customers.

If you were sloppy about your job, it showed in the presentation. The film might be scratched, or there might be loud
noises from lazy splices or even a picture that isn't centered on
the screen.

But if you cared about your job up in the projection booth,
you took pride in a print well built. You watched your builds
with confidence, knowing there wouldn't be splicing errors or
scratches.

In my experience, booth workers were about 50/50 on this,
where 50 percent truly cared about making sure the paying customers got a good show, and 50 percent were just in it for a
paycheck and made the rest of us look bad. By the way, that goes
for both union projectionists and "manager/operators," for what
it's worth. Lazy people can be found in all walks of life.

The first movie I ever built as a manager/operator projectionist was *Star Wars: A New Hope*, the 1997 rerelease.

I'd been on training for roughly two weeks and had only
watched one other movie be built from reel to platter. My
trainer, as he left the booth, said to me, "Don't fuck it up."

Now, I knew this was a trial by fire. He was tossing me to
the wolves to see how I responded to a challenge. And while I
was pretty sure a few mistakes would be allowed or forgiven,
I set about doing my absolute best to make this a perfect film
build.

And I continued a perfect record of movie-building and no
splice errors for years. Only once in my entire movie theater
career did I mis-splice a reel on a film, and even then it was
because the last sixteen frames of that reel were black and I just
miscounted.

From the beginning—because I was taught to—I cared about the film being built and projected correctly. Film fans deserved the best experience possible, and I strove to give them the experience I personally would want.

I built a lot of films that year, 1997: *As Good as It Gets, Liar Liar, Men in Black, Face/Off, L.A. Confidential, Good Will Hunting, Jackie Brown, Austin Powers, Grosse Pointe Blank*! These were the movies that defined me as a theater employee.

Sure, plenty of other films I would build later, like *The Sixth Sense* or *American Beauty*, would also be very impactful. But there's something nostalgic about that first year of being a projectionist—building films, screening films, running projectors, and ensuring a high-quality presentation. I can close my eyes and almost get high on the memory of it.

As CinemaSins has grown, I've found new appreciation for films I'd either dismissed, forgotten, or judged unfairly. Well, all except *The English Patient*. Fuck that movie. #ElaineWasRight

There's another thing that happens when you watch all the movies as a theater manager . . . and then you watch all the movies as a YouTube channel person. You start to get desensitized to things. Jump scares don't work as well. Common joke moments stand out and feel copied.

My wife and I watch movies together a lot, and she's always surprised when I lean over and say "That guy is evil" and I turn out to be right. It's not that I'm smart. It's just that I've seen too many movies.

A handful of films have been so difficult to find issues with that they have become memorable to me. *Inception* comes to mind. Christopher Nolan worked that script over and over, and there are very few questions a viewer can ask that the film doesn't answer.

We felt a similar frustration in writing sins for *Knives Out*, *District 9*, *Pulp Fiction*, or anything that is highly original and well thought out.

Very little about a sins video is actual criticism. Some of it is, of course, but most of it is just observational nitpickery. But every now and then a film comes along that makes the sin job so hard, you are obligated to walk away from the experience with more respect for it.

Jeremy, entirely too happy, 3 years old, 1978

Jeremy, 1st Grade, 1981

Baseball Jeremy, 5th Grade, 1985

Jeremy, with 4H blue-ribbon-winning cat, Scamper, 1986

Jeremy, meeting Optimus Prime in person, 1985

Jeremy and Josh goofing off at Billy Bob's in Ft. Worth, TX, 2002

Dodgers game, good seats, 2014

Redwoods at Muir Woods, San Francisco, 2014

Giants game, San Francisco, 2014

Jeremy, Kevin, and Chris, NHL playoffs, Chicago vs. Nashville, Chicago, IL, 2015

Jeremy at the White House, Washington, DC, 2016

Suite at Predators game, Chris arrives early, 2017

Wizard World interview: Jay Mewes, Bryan O'Halloran, Chris, Jeremy, Aaron, and Barrett, Nashville, TN, 2017

Leonard and Jessie Maltin, Jeremy, and Chris, Los Angeles, 2018

NYC business trip: Barrett, Jeremy, Chris, and Kevin, 2018

Hamilton stage, pre-show, 2018

Jeremy goofing around with fans at the first-ever SinWeek conference, Nashville, TN, 2019

The CinemaSins team screens a sins video premiere for fans at SinWeek, Nashville, TN, 2019

CHAPTER 8

My History of Nitpicking

My father's favorite shows when I was growing up were *Perry Mason*, *Matlock*, and *Murder, She Wrote*—all shows about murder. Remember, my father was a preacher. But I don't think he was attracted to the murder aspect; I think he enjoyed the justice of it all. I'm purely guessing, of course, because I never asked him about it. But those shows always found the real bad guy at the end, and the innocent guy went free. That and the intellect, the necessary cunning to outsmart a legal opponent.

Anyway, I was allowed to watch them with him from as early as I can remember, because these shows offered no swearing, no on-screen violence, and nothing offensive to PG audiences in terms of visuals. But each of them delved deep into discussion about murder, including methods, motives, weapons, and defenses.

"How deep was the stab wound, officer?" "We know the shooter stood there, because of the blood spatter pattern on the wall." "They definitely had sex before he killed her."

It was okay for me to hear people discussing murders weekly, but it wasn't okay for me to go see even PG-rated movies in the theater. That always seemed odd to me.

It also underscores America's weird problem with nudity despite its causal acceptance of violence.

Anyway, because I was raised in a very conservative, religious home, every single cassette tape I owned in high school—yes, I'm old and owned cassette tapes—was a Christian band or artist, except for the *Untouchables* soundtrack and some Bill Cosby stand-up comedy tapes—which, yes, that shit is now hilariously ironic as an "allowed" form of audio entertainment.

I was also a Bible Quizzer for eight years, first as a child in Children's Quizzing and then as a teen in Teen Quizzing. Here's Bible Quizzing in a nutshell: Every year they pick a different book of the Bible, and monthly they have trivia contests about that book. For the kids, everyone gets to answer, and it's multiple choice, because kids are losers.

For the teens, it's a jump-off. So they put these dollar-bill-sized "pads" on the chairs, and you sit on them. The Quizmaster (actual title, I wish I was making this up) asks the trivia question, and whenever you think you know the answer, even mid-question, you "jump" and lift your ass off the sensor pad.

The entire system is electronically rigged to a lighting console in front of the Quizmaster, so that raw math tells him which quizzer actually jumped first. Then that person gets a chance to answer the question.

So it becomes a contest of knowing the material better than your foes so that you can jump earlier and earlier without even needing to hear the end of the question.

And I'll be honest, because I'm kind of making fun of my own quizzing background, but I want to be clear: these kids know their shit. They study hard, and sometimes at national levels, these kids are jumping on the third word of the trivia question and still getting the answers right.

I was one of them. My final four years, my high school years, I literally memorized the book of the Bible we were quizzing on that year. That's ... borderline obsessive. Who memorizes fucking First and Second fucking Timothy?! Who does that?!

But Bible Quizzing also introduced me to a glorious concept: the Challenge. My parents always encouraged debate and discussion at the dinner table, but it was the Bible quizzing challenge that truly taught me to damn the man and fight for my perspective.

Each quizzing team had a captain and a cocaptain. And because sometimes these things are judgment calls made by humans, a team's captain was allowed to challenge a ruling if he or she thought it was made in error. You could challenge your opponent's correct ruling or your own incorrect ruling.

A challenge consisted of the captain standing, walking to the mic, and saying, "I challenge that ruling," followed by a one-minute argument. I loved it immediately.

The captain made their case for why the ruling should be overturned.

Then the other teams' captains had a chance to offer a rebuttal, and suddenly Bible Quizzing was academic bowl and debate club all rolled into one, and I was born for this shit. You could say I was raised for it, during years of Sunday School classes that ultimately boiled down to the teacher asking "Who knows this thing about this Bible story?" And I, being the preacher's kid, had heard said story dozens of times already and *always* knew the right answer first.

Anyway, the Quizmaster also had a helper, called a Content Judge. They were there to double-check answers and serve as a backup to the Quizmaster. After a challenge and rebuttal, the Quizmaster and Content Judge would confer and ultimately render a ruling either upholding the original or overturning it. And let me tell you, once you find a tiny loophole technicality and challenge a ruling only to have it overturned in your favor, you feel like Jesus himself, or maybe Perry Mason. Regardless, you get a thirst for nitpicking, challenging authority, and exploiting loopholes.

If you're me, you eventually develop a bit of a reputation as being a challenge-loving argue-puss. Or so I was told. I didn't care. I won most of my challenges, and I began to like making arguments—especially whenever I was able to be funny or snarky in the process.

One of my favorite shows in my teenage years was *Star Trek: The Next Generation*. This was my mother and my aunt's fault. Both huge Trek fans, they had introduced us to the movies and the old episodes when we were kids.

But *Next Generation* did exactly what it tried to do ... it took one generation's property and tweaked it just enough for the next generation of kids to fall for it on their own terms. I fucking loved it. I saw the new episodes and the reruns, and then my friend who had taped every single episode on VHS—in order!—gave me his collection, and I watched and rewatched those tapes until they fell apart.

Then one Christmas during high school, my older brother got me *The Nitpicker's Guide for Next Generation Trekkers*. The book, clearly written by a passionate fan who'd spent years watching the show over and over, spells out episode-by-episode all the mistakes and continuity errors the show contained.

Here's what most people misunderstand about CinemaSins, and what my parents at first misunderstood about the *Star Trek* nitpicker book. It's not about complaining. It's not even about fixing. It's about being so observant you notice things that even the creators of the show didn't see when they were making it. It's about a level of dedication and fandom that makes you obsessive—because you love what you're watching so much that your mind gravitates to find the "only" or the "only few" faults contained therein.

The book made me go back to the *Next Generation* episodes again and again—as I believe the CinemaSins videos drive viewers back to movies over and over. It's a celebration of uber-fandom and detail-observant viewing *because* there's an underlying love of the thing being nitpicked.

———◆———

In college, what followed was a love for *Mystery Science Theater 3000*, a show that made fun of bad older films in real time, with hecklers in the audience lobbing jokes at the screen. I couldn't get enough of it. The worse the movie, the more hilarious their jokes were.

It aired on Comedy Central, and I watched every episode I could.

When they changed hosts, I didn't care. I kept watching and kept laughing. Making fun of movies—riffing them, roasting them, AKA sinning them—was likely brought to life with *Mystery Science Theater 3000.*

I'm positive people mocked movies in real time before *MST3K,* maybe even in group settings, but no one took it mainstream until they came along. In a great many ways, CinemaSins wouldn't exist if *MST3K* hadn't paved the way.

When they finally released a proper film in cinemas, for their riffs on *This Island Earth,* Josh and I drove seventy-five minutes all the way to downtown Chicago to the *only* theater in all of Illinois that was playing it, and we both nearly peed from laughter while watching it.

We used to joke that we were paid to watch movies before they opened, but most of us—all the manager/operators, at least—were salaried anyway. So we were being paid, even if only technically speaking.

Chris and I worked together at a theater with twenty-seven screens. As you can guess, that meant a lot of coming and going of films every week.

Some Thursday nights, we'd have as many as seven to ten brand-new prints that needed to be previewed. So we'd enlist other managers and hourly staff, and watching Thursday night movies became a bit of a weekly celebration and respite from the grind. For a time, it was pretty sweet. I think, at some point, someone brought a girlfriend, and there was a blowjob, and then some rules got handed down from on high.

In the early 2000s, Regal banned any employee from attending a Thursday night screening *other* than the person that built it.

We just ignored that rule and kept letting employees watch preview screenings. Fuck corporate. Nearly every rule they gave us was designed to cover their own asses from some kind of lawsuit.

And things went great. We got all newly built prints watched for mistakes, and employees and managers alike got to see movies the night before they opened. It was perfect . . . until . . . dun dun dun . . . the age of digital arrived.

Digital film removed the need to build a print *and* the need to preview a newly built print to check for mistakes. So now no one could see new movies the night before they opened. And it was slightly after my time, but I'm told it Sucked with a capital S.

By the time YouTube was exploding, around 2009–2011, Chris and I had begun thinking about starting a channel of our own. We loved movies, thought ourselves generally funny, and wanted to be part of the gold rush.

We failed several times before coming up with the concept for CinemaSins.

The first video hit the home page of Buzzfeed, and our channel grew quite rapidly after that.

Even our early failed channels were also about nitpicking movies, just in different ways than the Sins format we eventually landed on. All along, we were just taking what we were (cinema nerds) and mixing it with what we liked (*MST3K*) to try and find something new.

In a way, you could say that I was destined to be a professional nitpicker.

But also that would be stupid and wrong. Destiny can suck my ass. You are what you make of yourself, for good or ill.

At most, I think you could say the environments I found myself in during formative years helped make me feel comfortable making jokes about almost any subject, and my love of movies came along . . . and CinemaSins was born.

CHAPTER 9

Paramount Call/Visit

In the fall of 2013 we published a sins video for an action movie from Paramount. A handful of weeks later, I got an email from a Paramount assistant asking for my phone number. A couple hours later my phone rang, and I was asked to hold, please, for the president of the studio.

Why yes, I did nearly soil my jeans, yes. Thank you for asking.

"Jeremy!" he barked when he came on the line. "Fucking hilarious! I saw that sins video you made, and you brought up everything we discussed when we were making that movie!"

He invited us out for a meeting and a studio tour after the holidays, and we, obviously, said yes. We set up a few other meetings and were off to LA in January of 2014.

Now this was going to be my first time in Los Angeles. I'd been in Orange County once, and that shit does not count. So I was excited. We decided to blow it out.

We flew first class, a decision I have regretted ever since because—as dumb as it sounds—the hot towels, extra leg room, and free alcohol have absolutely ruined me for coach. The anxiety when I travel gets pretty bad, largely because I have so little control over my own environment. In coach, so tight and cramped, it's a panic attack half the time. But in first class, sad as it is, I am *much* less anxious. I attribute this to the extra personal space, the hot towel, and, of course, the free booze.

I'd flown first class for all of twenty minutes when I fell hopelessly in love with it. I'm fortunate to be able to afford it, and I don't take that for granted—because first class is an absolute rip-off. Someday I am sure I will again be left to travel in coach or not at all, and I hope by then the doctors will have increased my Xanax dosage.

We researched the hotels the celebrities liked to stay at and booked a couple bungalows at the Sunset Marquis. Google it, it's amazing. There were a few contenders, but we really loved the "oasis" feel of this place. It's just off Sunset in West Hollywood, and we only had to walk a few blocks to see some kind of familiar landmark or location.

This was a wild and fun trip. The Paramount visit was the main reason for going, but our manager had scheduled some meetings and then had to leave town before we did. So Chris and I had a good bit of time to explore Los Angeles.

Day one, coming out of the hotel, we got in the car, and there in front of us, Kevin Fucking Costner got out of a sky-blue little Porsche and casually strolled into the Sunset Marquis. I only saw him one other time when we passed in the lobby, but I saw that Porsche every day we were there, parked literally in the very best spot on the street, just waiting for Kevin.

I chose to believe he was in town to promote a movie or do reshoots, because I'd read he had a huge ranch in Montana or some such state. I was still surprised he didn't have his own Los Angeles pad to crash in for a few days. Maybe he does, but it was being fumigated. I'll never know.

But I stayed in the same hotel as Kevin Costner. I breathed the same air, ate the same room service, showered in the same kind of ginormous waterfall room—seriously, you should stay at the Sunset Marquis just once, if only to take a shower. I'm not even fucking joking. It's ridiculously expensive and targeted at the rich and famous, but those showers don't fuck around. People in Heaven don't shower as good as the guests at the Sunset Marquis.

Anyway, Chris and I had some free time pretty early on that day, so we decided to rent a car and drive around. We went first up into the Hollywood Hills, wondering if we were driving by any famous peoples' homes ... or at least a Kardashian home. The drive up into the hills was steep and winding, with excessive wealth on display no matter which window you looked out of.

We decided to visit Griffith Observatory and gawk at the Hollywood sign. The Griffith Observatory is a *much* more popular place than movies would have you believe. In the movies it's always empty so Transformers can meet in private or so romantics can dance in the planetarium. In person it's thirty school groups at once and a constant hum of noise that only comes when thousands of kids are in once place at the same time.

We parked and started walking, and I immediately got in trouble with a cop for smoking.

Okay, brief aside, I used to smoke cigarettes. I don't anymore, because Ray Liotta's favorite drug, Chantix, is a fucking miracle of a thing and I quit quite easily with that medicine's help. And no, the Chantix people did NOT pay me to say that. I wish they would, to be honest.

But back when I was a smoker, I always got in trouble for smoking in the wrong places. Apparently the observatory grounds were smoke-free—probably because of their proximity to the Hollywood Hills where wildfires are common. I didn't even think twice about it, which is pretty ugly on my part, and I was properly shamed.

But even when it wasn't cigarette-related, it seemed that anytime Chris and I traveled somewhere, I would always get in trouble and yelled at by some authority figure.

In Chicago I leaned too close to some expensive merch on the C2E2 expo floor. We were there visiting with our friend Doug, the Nostalgia Critic, at his booth. So the asshole in the next booth over yelled at me for leaning on a pole near his glass display cases. He was a total jerk about it, as I hadn't even so much as jostled his table or his wares even a tiny bit. But he acted like I was using the metal divider pole as a pommel horse. So I came *this* close to buying something from him and just smashing it on the floor in front of him out of spite. But I didn't. Some things are funny ideas in the moment but only make you grow regretful as time passes. That would have been one of those.

Anyway, the Griffith Observatory was cool, in that "kind of a pain in the ass to get there and back" kind of way. But we did get to drive through the tunnel they shot *Back to the Future Part II*'s big Biff/hoverboard sequence in. That was cool. Pretty sure we drove by a Kardashian house as well. I mean ... the odds are so good I figure we had to have.

We met up with our manager to go to a meeting with Soul Pancake—the online content company created by Rainn Wilson. Nothing ever came of that meeting, but they were all super friendly people. Lots of Post-it notes on walls in that office too. We did not get to meet Mr. Wilson.

That night we decided at the last minute to go to a Clippers game. The tickets were cheap because the team wasn't great that year, so we spent under thirty bucks on seats seven rows behind one of the goals. We're 99 percent sure we spotted Dodgers slugger Matt Kemp on the first row.

And we had a blast. The Clippers were hosting the Wizards, and I came away with a few concrete revelations: John Wall is hugely underrated and moves like the wind, the NBA is ten times better in person than on TV, and also we parked so far from the stadium that my legs ground half to dust by the time we got back to that fucking Prius.

The next day was the big Paramount visit.

Fortunately, we'd spent the previous night getting fucking blasted in the bar downstairs, and by "fortunately" I obviously mean the opposite. So I spent the morning puking, between hits of Coke to try and dim the caffeine headache that was bouncing off my skull like a Rage Against the Machine song.

Paramount, like most studios, I assume, was pretty secure. We sat at the gate a few moments while security checked our credentials and then told us exactly where to park. Like ... exactly where to park. Then we were escorted to the building where most of the studio execs keep offices.

Up first was the big meeting. We sat in an impressive two-story waiting room for about twenty minutes before being called upstairs. Unfortunately, the studio president who'd loved our video and called me personally was unexpectedly gone for the day. We were instead meeting with two top producers.

Now, to Paramount's credit, they sent in two massively successful and prolific film producers to speak with us. While we were bummed not to meet the president, we were pleased as punch to meet these two men.

For the most part, the meeting went about as you would expect. An hour or so of professional and polite discourse about film and our YouTube channel.

I remember one of the men asked, "How do you get the movie in order to make the video?" I suppose he was wondering if we were using torrents. We weren't. "We buy the Blu-ray," I said. "So . . . at least you're making a little money off of us."

I immediately regretted saying it, but it was too late.

Twenty minutes later the other producer mentioned a movie he'd worked on, and Chris immediately said, "That was a terrible movie." Chris didn't say it mean. He said it gently, even. He just said it like a fact. And honestly, the movie in question is terrible. The producer even smiled and told us a couple stories about working on that terrible film.

I guess if I'm being honest, I expected some kind of offer from them at that meeting. Not anything massive, but maybe just a pledge to communicate on future Paramount videos and maybe work together to help us avoid claims or help promote future films.

But there was nothing like that. We talked for an hour with

two legit Hollywood producers—which was awesome—and then they handed us off to a tour guide.

And a tour on a film studio lot is an amazing thing. Each studio is different, I'm sure. But we saw Dr. Phil's studio, we saw LL Cool J's purple Lamborghini, or Porsche, or whatever it was. It was definitely slick and purple. We were told he was filming for *NCIS: Los Angeles* inside at the moment.

We saw the Forrest Gump bench and the sloped parking lot and painted wall that had been used to create the Red Sea in *The Ten Commandments*, and we literally walked right by Jim Parsons.

We got to see film memorabilia, like the jacket Tom Cruise wore in *War of the Worlds*. And even though I'm probably the thousandth person to tell you this, Tom Cruise is a tiny man. I've seen puppets that jacket wouldn't fit.

We got to see the original Desilu office buildings and hear the story about how Lucille Ball basically singlehandedly saved *Star Trek* and *Mission Impossible*. We saw the studio-theater lobby, which was used as a setting for a bank in *Clear and Present Danger*.

But then ... then we went off-tour, and we were shown a section of the studio lot that most folks never get to see: the archive. Inside were the master copies for every Paramount film ever. Many were in dual film canisters broken down by reel—the same way I used to receive new movies in theaters to build and show audiences.

But these labels had titles like *The Godfather*, *The Hunt for Red October*, *Chinatown*, *Airplane!*, *Rear Window*, *Psycho*, *Apocalypse Now*, *Raiders of the Lost Ark* ... my GOD. Row after row of iconic films, so close I could touch them—the master prints. This was like a guest trip to film projection Heaven, and God was asking me to thread up one of his favorite films for a viewing.

I have heard people tell me about the Grand Canyon, using words I myself have employed regarding the redwoods in California: you have to see it to believe it. It's a spiritual experience.

This film archive of master prints was the Grand Canyon, but if it was full of redwood trees, Easter Island statues, pyramids, and pirate gold. I could smell the history. And I don't mean that flippantly. Maybe I'm exaggerating slightly, but old-school real film stock has a certain smell that can't be duplicated.

They would never let me thread up these pieces of film history, nor should they, but standing that close . . . I couldn't help daydreaming about piecing together the reels of *The Hunt for Red October*, careful on every splice . . . and then watching in the screening room the original fucking master print of that movie. Religious people could get a tour of Heaven by St. Peter himself and not feel more "behind the curtain" luck than we did in that Paramount vault.

I could have stayed in that room for days. The history. The stories. The magic. Master copies of all these iconic films, a few inches from me. It's probably as close as I'll personally ever get to Heaven, that's for sure.

I thought nothing would top that Paramount tour, until we spotted Joaquin Phoenix in the restaurant inside the Sunset Marquis.

Keep in mind, this was a hotel we are spending several hundred dollars a night on, and this restaurant is in the very damn center of it all.

So after spotting Joaquin in the early evening, we decided to go in for a drink. We ask the hostess for a couple seats at the bar, and this girl deadpans, "We're all full up."

I literally laughed out loud in her face, a mere few yards from Joaquin Phoenix himself.

The restaurant was empty save for the famous guy and his guest. So only one of two things was possible. Either Joaquin told the restaurant to keep everyone out, or else the restaurant decided to keep everyone out of their own accord.

If it's the former, then Joaquin big-timed us like an A-lister. If it's the latter, then who is the person at the Sunset Marquis that makes the decision on which celebrities are "close the entire restaurant" worthy and which are not? Also, when you draw that line, do you really draw it in such a way that Joaquin Phoenix finds himself above that line?

I mean, in 2019, post-*Joker*, sure ... he's that level of star. But in 2014, coming off the film *Her*—which is excellent, and he is excellent in it—it's a stretch that he's that big of a star.

I'm just saying, Kevin Costner didn't big-time me out of any restaurants during *his* stay at the Sunset Marquis. But for Joaquin it was all, "Please clear the restaurant for Mr. Phoenix to take a meal."

Granted, we *did* only want to go in and have a drink so we could sideways gawk at him. And (sigh) that's probably something he gets a lot. So maybe he gets tired of it and sometimes a bar or restaurant helps him avoid it all by just pretending they are full when they are empty. He might even pay extra for the privilege. I certainly don't know.

But listen, it just makes a better story if he's big-timing people left and right.

CHAPTER 10

VidCon and San Fran

We went to VidCon in 2014. It was our first and only time attending the convention, and we had a good enough time, but it was ... strange.

I sat on a panel about advertising on YouTube, and it was fun enough, though the crowd was sparse. I ended up getting quoted in an article in the *Los Angeles Times* about the state of advertising on YouTube, because the reporter had been in the audience. Ha! Quoted by the *Los Angeles Times* ... how many of your friends can say that?

We saw Wil Wheaton on the expo floor the first day and geeked out. He walked by, and we said nothing because we were starstruck.

But VidCon is mostly about singers and vloggers, the makeup artists and the life coaches of YouTube—the people on camera for every video. Almost no one knew what we looked like. We were even wearing CinemaSins shirts, and only a few people came up to us and asked if we were CinemaSins.

Which is fine. We didn't go to be mobbed by fans. (We absolutely went for that reason and were crushed it didn't happen.) We went to experience the event. This was billed as the biggest YouTuber conference around. And I guess it is, but not super useful for all kinds of YouTubers.

I do remember, vividly, going out for a steak dinner with Chris that first night and getting a little tipsy on wine and telling him that CinemaSins absolutely *had* to have been created by both of us, and that neither of us alone could ever have done it. That we share a lot in common but we get on each other's nerves sometimes, but our differences are what makes the videos great. I meant it all, even if I was drunk. Because it was all true.

We made some good contacts at VidCon—we even had a great conversation with the original Ask A Ninja guy! But the event was geared more toward fans and face-famous creators. You can barely walk through any section of VidCon without having a fan eruption kind of moment, where someone recognizes a hot YouTuber and hundreds of screams go up as fans chase after that person for pictures and autographs. Chaos is the baseline for VidCon.

By the last day, we ditched.

We hit a Dodgers game—a first for both of us. What a ballpark. What an experience. So casual, yet fully engaged. The liveliest and most fun sports crowd I've ever encountered. But it is an absolute pain in the fucking ass to get there. My God. Like rush hour in Boston, only somehow with more honking and middle fingers.

The Dodgers were playing the San Francisco Giants that

night, and both teams were good that year, in contention for the playoffs. So the game was good. I remember eating a Dodger Dog, which was basically like any ballpark hot dog (delicious), only it was over a foot long (righteous). Eventually the game ended and it was time for dinner. We had reservations.

So we took a SUPER expensive fucking cab ride to Century City, because I was gonna eat at Tom Colicchio's restaurant, Craft, if it was the last thing I did in LA. As a huge fan of *Top Chef*, I'd made eating at Craft a bucket list event, and boy howdy, kids, did it live up to the hype. Amazing. Service so tight it felt like a movie. Impeccable in every way. (I feel compelled to tell you that this book is not in any way sponsored or funded by Craft, Tom Colicchio, *Top Chef*, or Bravo TV, but it really should be, if we're being honest.)

I've been to LA twice since then, and I've eaten at Craft both times, and on one of my two New York City trips I also ate at the NYC outpost of Craft—the original Craft. It was hands down the best dining experience I've ever had. All four times. It's not cheap, but it's worth every penny. The service, the food, the ambience, all first rate. I mean . . . God. Damn.

I recommend the short rib and the whipped Yukon gold potatoes, but the menu changes all the time. Just go. Just save for weeks or months and go. Or sell a child or two . . . and just go!

After dinner we bought an even more expensive cab ride from Century City back to Anaheim. There was traffic, but the high from the meal and the wine we'd drunk with the meal gave the hour-plus ride a dreamlike quality. I remember thinking it felt like I was in the movie *Drive* and Ryan Gosling was my chauffeur.

When we got to the hotel, the cab driver turned out to be one of those "I suddenly don't take a credit card" guys. This is a known scam. Somehow the taxi companies fuck over their drivers regarding credit cards, and whenever they get cash they end up with a bigger cut. So some of them turn to lies and pranks to get cash out of you. "My machine broke just this morning," this guy said.

Chris, who'd lived in New York City for a few years, wasn't having it. However, I was buzzed and full and tired—and at this point was unaware of the common scam—so I went inside and got cash from an ATM. I remember Chris telling me, "Don't give him cash!" But I did it anyway. Sometimes exhaustion trumps morality lessons.

The next morning we paid a van driver $90 to drive us from Anaheim to LAX, and we got there with plenty of time to spare. Waiting in an airport is the worst. There is a constant buzz of crowd noise, punctuated by the constant speaker announcements. You can't concentrate on anything.

We grabbed some snacks and drinks and settled in near our eventual gate. I was reading a book in the chairs outside our gate when Chris elbowed me, then pointed casually in front of us. I looked up to see Adrian Grenier walking past us. He strolled up to the gate desk, then stood to the side for a few minutes.

Now, we were still flying first class at this point because . . . why not? First class rules. Actually first class is great for early boarding and deboarding, in addition to the free alcohol. But I've covered all this already.

Anyway, we ended up literally right behind Adrian Grenier, star of *Entourage*. Star of *The Devil Wears Prada* and that one

Sabrina movie about the Britney Spears song! This plane was going nonstop from Los Angeles to Nashville, TN. So Vincent Chase was going to our hometown!

My first idea was to tweet him publicly, "Yo, we are literally right behind you." Chris helped me realize that such a tweet might come off more stalker-like than I intended. And also make for an awkward five-hour flight for all involved.

We did ultimately tweet him that we were on the same plane as him. He tweeted that he was going to Nashville to see a band in concert that was signed to his record label. He also suggested we should sin his movie about the paparazzi, called *Teenage Paparazzo*.

We accepted the challenge on Twitter but then never followed through—though largely this was because *Teenage Paparazzo* had not yet received a Blu-ray release, and we didn't want to create a video from the DVD. In our defense, we *hate* putting out a sins video using only a DVD copy of a film, which has poor resolution for the modern audience.

But this much I know for sure: dude was on his phone the entire flight, and his thumbs and fingers move like lightning. I couldn't see well enough to see his screen—not that I was looking—but his fingers and thumbs worked that phone for the entire flight, and he got shit done. He was Insta-ing or tweeting or texting or emailing the entire time. Man, the man is . . . nonstop.

Also worth noting: he didn't bring a lick of luggage. Not even a bag or backpack. Just flew halfway across the country with the clothes on his back. That's a baller. I would never be brave enough to do that. Sure, I could buy new underwear and a new shirt, but flying with *nothing*?

Later that same year, our former employer ReelSEO.com was putting on a video marketing conference in San Francisco, and we were asked to come and speak. This was a quick trip, less than two days, but we packed it the fuck out with activities.

We arrived in the afternoon the first day and had time to check in and then go for dinner. We walked through Chinatown to a restaurant called Coi. There was no menu and no prices. You just eat what they make that day and then pay for it. We were psyched.

Eleven courses came and went. Some were unforgettable, like the smoked egg yolk topped with caviar or the watermelon cucumber soup with spot prawn. Other dishes were gross to me, like the ones with the raw fish and the squishy thing. Overall we both had a great time, largely because we'd said yes when the waiter asked if we wanted the alcohol pairing for every course.

So we ate and ate, and most of it was amazing, honestly. The whole time a couple next to us was getting closer and closer to fucking under the table with their feet, talking loudly and being annoying. I didn't care, I was eating fancy-ass food and drinking WINE PAIRINGS, fools! I was over the moon!

I remember this was the first time I ever had a rosé that I liked.

Then we got the bill. Nine hundred fucking dollars. We laughed for maybe five minutes straight, because, of course, we were drunk as fuck. Thankfully we had enough money to pay that bill and enough even still to afford a cab ride home, since we were wasted to hell and back.

The next day, we had a quick thing at the conference, then

we had two free hours, then we had a thing at the conference midafternoon, then we were free the rest of the night.

So we did the early thing, which turned out to be an interview on stage while all the attendees of the conference were eating lunch. The interview went fine, and in the end we were asked to "sin" the very conference we were attending, which we gave a valiant effort toward before joking our way out of it quickly.

Then I declared, "Let's go see the redwoods!"

My brother had recently been to the Grand Canyon, and he had told me to put it on my bucket list and push it to the top, telling me I could never understand it until I saw it.

That's the redwoods as well, people.

Now, I still haven't been to the Grand Canyon, but it's at the top of my list. But I am now telling everyone I know to go see the redwoods, like some kind of crazed cultist. "You HAVE to see the redwoods!"

The redwoods aren't something a picture will ever do justice. You show people a picture you took in Muir Woods and they'll say, "Wow, big tree." You can't comprehend the scope and scale until you see them in person. They were more than I ever dreamed they'd be.

And we only had two hours. So we had to rent a car, and an SUV is all they had, so it cost more. Immediately I realized I could not drive over the Golden Gate Bridge due to my gripping fear of crashing off of bridges into bodies of water. Chris was all like, "I'll drive, I guess, but I'm not exactly excited about driving over this bridge either."

San Francisco traffic sucks balls, so it took us nearly forty-five minutes to get out to Muir Woods and park way the hell down the street. We walked for ten minutes, and we then had maybe twenty-five minutes to spend with the giant trees before we had to head back.

Best twenty-five minutes ever. I'm serious.

Imagine standing at the base of the Sears Tower—sorry, Willis Tower—and you look up at the top, only instead of a building, it's a fucking tree. That's . . . the redwoods.

The expense of the rental and the annoyance of the traffic and the tight timeline . . . all worth it. Worth it times two. Worth it forever. I fell in love with those trees. Good God, you do not know how big a fucking tree can be if you've never seen a redwood. I want to start a nonprofit that raises money just to send people to see the redwoods. You see a tree that big and you realize how much of a mosquito your life is in the grand scheme of things.

We raced back, fighting even more traffic and vertigo—the feeling, not the movie—and returned the rental car inside of two hours. They legitimately looked shocked to see us. Like, who rents a car for only two hours? We do, bitches.

We raced to the hotel—on foot—and we did the next thing, which turned out to be a quick interview, and then we were done.

Then Chris said, "I just got tickets to a baseball game, let's go." And so we went.

Interestingly, the game featured the local Giants and the in-state rivals, the Los Angeles Dodgers—it would be a rematch of the game we'd seen just a month prior in LA.

We had great seats in left field, and they have some of the best stadium food I've tasted.

And it was a fun game—Tim Lincecum pitched like ass, but that is a gorgeous fucking ballpark. Probably the nicest park I'd ever been to until I finally got to see Camden Yards in Baltimore a few years later. Still, a great place to watch a baseball game.

Problem was, we'd walked. And I had recently developed a bit of a sciatic thing that gets exacerbated when I stand or walk too much. Now, Chris, he walked like a motherfucker. He walked all over Nashville sometimes just for fun, exercise, or to finish a podcast episode he was listening to. The dude loves to walk.

But our hotel and the ballpark were 1.5 miles apart. And we walked both ways. I mean, we didn't know it was that far when we decided to walk it, but that distance wouldn't have stopped him.

And all I'm saying is I nearly died. But Chris was patient as I paused every block for a brief rest.

That night I woke with such sudden leg cramps that I flailed myself out of bed completely, smacking my ankle into the dresser.

That morning, the ankle pain was massive, but I still looked forward to our breakfast before the flight out. But then I ate the breakfast and got sick in the restaurant bathroom, and at that point I just wanted to fucking go home.

CHAPTER 11

Actionable YouTube Advice for Creators

Here it is. The chapter I promised you. The chapter full of actionable advice about YouTube from me to you.

Some of you skipped ahead to get here, and I just hope you eventually go back and read what you jumped over, because it's hysterical and all about your mom.

Anyway . . . In mostly-random order . . .

Follow the YouTube Creator Playbook

I realize it's a document created by "the man," and therefore you have a faint innate distrust. Some of you might even think You-Tube hates small creators in favor of large brands. All I can tell you is that people thought that back in 2012 when we started CinemaSins, and we followed the YouTube Creator Playbook as closely as possible.

You will read it and wonder what the big deal is, because so much of it is common sense. But it still works. "Put keywords you think your video should be searchable for in your title." I mean . . . duh, right? But a *ton* of creators don't do that.

It's got almost all the advice I could give you, but I'm going to lay out a few specific ones I would underline.

Create and Follow a Schedule

Pick a day and time for your videos to be published, whether it's weekly or monthly. Pick a schedule and then stick to it. This is the easiest way to build loyal viewers because you train them to expect new content.

Be careful here, and don't overextend yourself. Burnout on YouTube is real, and in some cases even feeling depression and anxiety—like me!—is too.

"Stick to a schedule" also doesn't mean you can never take a break or miss an upload here and there. Think of it like television; sometimes you tune in to your favorite show and it's a rerun and there's no new episode. Life happens. Leave room for life.

Choose Content/Title that Inspires Debate or Discourse

When we were creating CinemaSins's first video, we had lots of discussions about the name and how to title the videos. At first we thought about phrasing around the word "mistakes." But pretty quickly we realized it would be better to make the things we are listing *sound* negative, but from a definition standpoint, be more vague.

So we went with "sins." But in titling the video, we decided to go harsh, with "Everything Wrong With." And even the word "wrong" is subjective, but still has a common meaning of "bad."

We could have listed great things about movies, and done "Everything Right With," and, in fact, others have actually done that. But it would never have gained the initial viral traction without the controversial-sounding video titles. It instantly draws lines among viewers between those that hate the movie and those that love it. Debate is near instantaneous.

Pay Attention to Your Data

It's important to look at who is watching, and when, and from where, and for how long. You can pinpoint specific things you are doing that the audience particularly loves or hates and make valuable changes to future content.

Believe me, there is actionable data in your YouTube statistics that I'd guess 85 percent of YouTubers don't even know about.

Think Long-Term

You need more than one viral hit video if you want to have a career on YouTube or make any kind of recurring revenue.

I hear a lot of channel ideas from a lot of people in person and online, and way too many of them are far too specific. You need something that is repeatable, and the best way to get there is to start with something you know, or at least know a lot about.

For Chris and me, it was movies. It was always movies. All our failed channels before CinemaSins were movie related. Not that we are movie experts or reviewers professionally—never claimed to be—but we have watched a lot of movies and have a lot of information and opinions regarding film. Enough to make for repeatable content.

Hustle for Coverage

Influencers on social media can make or break a YouTube channel. Do research on your video's target audience. Is it a video of a guy riding a downhill mountain bike race only to fall spectacularly? Well, that's going to interest bikers, for sure. Athletes in general, I'd imagine. Also folks that like fail videos or bloopers.

Now ... time to research where that kind of content is most often shared, and by whom. Which popular websites are sharing lots of fail videos? Who are some of the most influential mountain biking personalities online?

Don't forget, viral action can come offline as well, so don't be afraid to target television shows, local stations, newspapers, magazines, and other media in your pursuit for coverage.

Our method was deceptively simple. We just emailed a writer or editor at the outlet in question, briefly explained the video (in two sentences), and offered a link.

The first twelve to fifteen weeks that we did this, we got at least one hit for coverage every single time.

You have to remember that writers for websites, blogs, human interest publications, and so on are people who are just as desperate for a good story to highlight as you are for coverage. If you have a good enough piece of video content, and you target the right outlets carefully and politely, you can benefit from that constant need for more articles shared by most online publishers.

Find a Good MCN and Sign Up

MCN stands for "multi-channel network." These are companies that represent many YouTube channels at once. As a result of their size, MCNs can get direct access to YouTube personnel.

They can also help deal with copyright claims—independent channels have a harder time fighting claims because the MCNs boast a reputation with YouTube and can "vouch" for a channel, whereas single-owner channels are left to fend off every claim and email by themselves.

What makes a good MCN? Man, you tell me. We've been with two in total. One was great but too long-distance for us to meet regularly. The other was great and in Nashville, so we meet all the time. Both companies helped us deal with copyright claims. Both companies helped us get higher CPM rates—which means cost per mile, or the price of a thousand ad impressions—for video ads. All alone on our own, we'd have never made it past the first year.

It's fine to go viral and manage things on your own. But if you want a YouTube channel that has long-term earnings potential, you need assistance. I've seen hundreds of channels have viral hit videos that even get them on *Ellen* or the national news, but the channel never gains many subscribers or grows at all beyond that first video—because they had no idea what to do with the sudden, huge new audience. An MCN will know what to do and can help you turn that rash of new viewers into long-term fans.

Cross Fingers, Toes, and Anything Else Crossable

The sad fact of the matter is that luck plays a major role in what YouTube channels get popular and which ones get ignored. We can give you all these tips—and I truly believe they all helped—but following every piece of advice we give won't guarantee you YouTube success.

I can give advice and offer tips, but I can't be getting sued by book readers who follow every step and still don't grow a large following. Luck is a part of it, and anyone telling you otherwise is lying.

Think about how easy it would have been for me to title this book with a promise of YouTube wealth, only to put an asterisk caveat somewhere in the small print . . . sucking in a ton of readers that believed the headline just to take their money and not give them the same return in entertainment? I could have done that shit with minimal blowback . . . and I'd have probably made ten times what this more-honest version of the book will make.

But I'm not a liar. Luck will influence whether or not your YouTube channel is successful. I'm sorry. It's just a fact.

That doesn't mean you shouldn't try. Quite the opposite. The more who try, the more who stand a chance to make it. Try often. Try various ideas. Try and try and try. We tried four times before CinemaSins hit it big as a YouTube channel.

Age-Old Marketing Techniques Still Apply

You've seen the YouTube video thumbnails with the girl in a bikini, and a video title suggesting something even more salacious, yes? While YouTube is working to stem and stop this kind of activity, it's a clear demonstration of an age-old marketing idea: sex sells. Or, to boil it down even further, that you can sell products by appealing to the very base natures of men and women.

For our channel, one focused on nitpicking movies, we simply focused on doing more female-targeted films in order to draw in more woman fans.

Don't Aim for a Career on YouTube

I get why it's tempting. And it does seem easy, and truly . . . it is. On the work side of things, at least. But there's so much luck involved that I've seen people go into debt buying video equipment because they are certain the videos they'll capture will be viral gold. And then they're not.

If you want a career on YouTube, do what Chris and I did. Start it off as a side project while you maintain another full-time job. And then if the channel grows, you can always quit the other job.

We failed several times before one of our channel ideas finally stuck and started growing subscribers and earning money. But before that happened, we both had other jobs to keep us afloat.

Claims and Monetization

I'm sure a lot of you are hoping for specific advice regarding copyright claims or video demonetization. I'll do the best I can.

Everything will go more smoothly if your channel is signed to an MCN.

The field on YouTube is entirely tilted toward copyright holders, and content creators are the ones with the consistent burden of defense or proof. So much so that some scammers falsely claim content and make tens of thousands of dollars while the dispute rages on.

For the uninitiated, the claims process works like this. A copyright holder finds a video using its source material—like our sins videos using movie footage. They give no thought at this point in the process to Fair Use, I assure you. So they claim the video as theirs. They can then block it, take all the ad money from it, or stop our ability to earn from it.

I don't know how deep you want to dive here, but there are manual claims, automated claims, and also manual claims that are automated but intended to look manual. All of these things kill a video's momentum or chances of being included in the recommended videos section.

So then we have the option to dispute the claim. Which we do. We have some legal speak in there about Fair Use. But the studio then has thirty days to even respond in any way. Thirty days we're not earning, not gaining video momentum, nothing. After thirty days, most studios reject our dispute and reassert their claim.

We dispute again, and then typically wait another thirty days before anything happens. At *that* point, the studio has two options: drop the claim or issue a takedown notice.

If they drop the claim, technically, the money is supposed to come back to us, having been held in escrow during the dispute. But that only happens about half the time. The rest of the time it disappears. Poof. Vapor money.

If they issue a takedown notice, then we either take them to court or remove the video.

Ninety-nine percent of claims end right here, with the studio dropping the claim. Because all studios employ lawyers, and 99 percent of the lawyers will tell them they will lose in court because our videos are Fair Use.

Music claims are a whole other animal. The music publishers are evil. Straight up, no lie, evil fucking bloodsucking assholes. They have written software that cruises around on YouTube looking for *any* match to the songs/music in their publishing catalog. Even one second long or less.

Then they claim the entire video's profits for themselves. For a half second of a rap song, we lost 100 percent of the revenue from a twenty-minute Sins video.

YouTube knows about this and are even trying to fight it, but they are losing, and they've been behind the whole time.

Core viewers will know we sometimes upload a rerelease sins video on Saturdays. Most of the time, this is a video with a few seconds of music—used in the movie itself or in our audio—where the publishing company is claiming all of our earnings. So we re-edit the video, cut the two seconds of whatever music it is, and re-upload. The fun thing there is that we get to relive all the movie studio claims we defeated the first time these videos were uploaded.

I would personally not advise anyone to start a YouTube channel using copyrighted footage or music, no matter how much it falls in line with the Fair Use guidelines. It's just too much of a headache. It will drive you crazy keeping up with and fighting claims, all the while dodging actual channel strikes, of which you only get three before your channel goes away permanently.

Now, as for the waves of channels on YouTube getting suddenly demonetized without warning, I can't help. It hasn't happened to us, and hopefully it won't. But plenty of innocuous channels have lost their ability to earn without warning or explanation, and it's truly frightening. Besides Chris and I, we employ four other people full-time. Those four are counting on our ability to earn from our videos in order for them to keep their jobs and provide for their families.

YouTube makes a highlight video every year about its creators—we're never in there—but it's mostly a marketing stunt designed to make creators think they are the first thing on YouTube's mind. When in reality, YouTube's mostly concerned with money, money, and money.

They will sell you out for a biscuit if the right megacorporation leans on them enough.

Pay Attention

Just look around. Find the places where popular videos get shared, and start watching them daily. Or even multiple times per day.

I'm talking about Wired, Buzzfeed, Uproxx, and definitely the /r/videos sub on reddit. Watch spaces like that, and do it for weeks.

Look at the daily YouTube list of Trending Videos for a while.

What trends can you spot? What types of videos are going viral, and why? What are audiences craving more of?

If you want YouTube success, you need to do the research ahead of time before you start your channel. It's either that, or you start five channels that suck and quit them before finally finding your groove, like we did.

I'd advise you to go the research route.

CHAPTER 12

The Masters and Getting Wasted in Chicago

Because of the success of the YouTube channel, I was making enough money to finally splurge on something. So for Christmas 2014, I gave my father and brother a stocking each, filled with a golf ball, binoculars, and a photograph . . . all symbolic, as I finally announced I was taking all three of us to the Masters that next year.

Now, when we were boys, Dad played a lot of golf. At that time in Indiana, and throughout a lot of the country, it was common for golf courses to let preachers play for free. I have no idea if that's still the case, but I always thought it was strange, even back then.

Usually my brother and I were just along for the ride. But once or twice a round, he'd let us each hit a shot for him, or after him.

We sucked, because we were untrained kids, but I'd fallen in love with the game. The practice shots he allowed us to take cemented my bond. I think it drove my brother away from the game, at least for high school and college. During and after college, he found a lot of his wife's family played golf, as did his business colleagues, so he started playing more.

I started early, playing entire "rounds" of golf in the backyard with plastic balls every afternoon. A tree or even a fire hydrant could be a "hole." I laid out an entire eighteen-hole course. I'd put electrical tape over parts of the plastic balls to cover some of the holes and give them more weight and distance. And I'd pick a real golfer I liked to be represented by each ball, and then I'd play a round—sometimes, on Sundays, even a full four-round tournament.

My freshman year of high school I tried out for the golf team. On day one the only experience I had was a few dozen shots on the course while Dad played over the years and backyard plastic golf. I topped the first drive, with everyone who was trying out looking on from behind me, and it went about twenty-five feet. Knowing nothing much about golf, I walked up and used the driver again to try and smack the ball out of the tall rough. It didn't go very far, and I immediately wanted to die.

Walking to the ball again, I remember thinking, "We have to move. We can't live here anymore."

And I wish I could tell you I turned it around that day. But I did not. I played nine holes of some of the worst golf you could imagine. I shot over sixty . . . on nine holes of golf.

But I had a natural swing, the coach said.

Tryouts lasted a few weeks, including spring break, and as

members of the golf team (for now), everyone that wanted to could play for free at our home course to practice. And I went every single day of spring break and played eighteen holes with my friend Andy, who was also trying out. It *snowed* two of those days—this was Northern Indiana, so March is still basically winter. Still we golfed.

And by the end of tryouts, I had improved enough to make the team. I played three years of high school golf, rising as high as the number two varsity player on the team my junior year, when I averaged a 72 score for the season.

I didn't play my senior year because my guidance counselor told me I had nearly enough credits to graduate after one semester of my senior year. I took a class at a local university to finish my credits, and boom . . . I was out of school five months ahead of every other high schooler I knew! It would have been sweet if I'd had anyone my age to hang out with. Point is, I didn't play golf that year competitively.

When I got to college, I learned the golf team had to do conditioning—running—as part of their training. Running? The golf team?

Now . . . I love golf. I love it. I think I maybe could have been really good at it. But I hate running more than I love anything. I hate running more than I love sex. I hate running more than I love runny eggs. Running fucking sucks, and people who do it for fun are probably serial killers in waiting.

So I quit competitive golf forever at that point and turned my extracurricular activities to . . . movies!

You guessed it was movies, right? You *are* actually reading this thing and not just skimming, right?

So I played golf regularly off and on over the years, getting progressively worse the less I played. I still love the game, both playing it and watching it, and a lot of that is because of my father's love of the game.

One year, while my brother, Jeff, was in college and I was in high school, my father arranged a golf weekend with one of *his* brothers, as well as my grandfather—Dad's dad. We went to Myrtle Beach and played three courses in two days, and it was amazing.

We all continued to play off and on in our own lives, and Jeff even attended the Memorial PGA event in Ohio several times.

But the ultimate golf-lover's event—at least for Americans—has to be the Masters. And we all loved golf enough to appreciate a trip together to that hallowed ground.

The Masters!!!

Now, at the time of the gift, I had not purchased tickets or passes. I had merely looked a bit on StubHub and figured I'd get the tickets later. They were going for about $500 per pass for a two-day thing. That was way doable, so I didn't think much about it.

But the Masters isn't like a regular baseball game. The tickets are almost all sold to club members, relatives of past champions, and longtime attendees.

Flash forward a few months, and I realize, "Oh shit, I need to buy those Masters tickets!" And the prices had gone up. Long story short, it cost a total of about $9,000 for the three of us to get into the tournament Saturday and Sunday. I bought through StubHub, and when we had passed the final checkpoint and gotten onto the actual Augusta National grounds, I literally said out loud, "I honestly wasn't sure that was going to work until just now."

But it did work. And for two days my brother and dad and I had the time of our lives. This was 2015, the year Jordan Spieth went wire to wire.

But Tiger also played, and I'd always had a connection with Tiger Woods. We were the same age, but he also represented the ideal of golf—that the mind really could triumph over the physical and psychological terrors of a golf course. That humans could be close to perfect on the golf course. And I was going to get to see him play in person—assuming he made the cut.

He did.

We set up our chairs in the pine brush forest on the par five, thirteenth hole. Fun fact: if you have a Masters chair, wherever you set it in the morning is your spot. Even if you put the chair there and wander off to watch action at another hole for hours on end, no one will sit in your chair or move it. It's Masters etiquette.

Etiquette is a big fucking deal at the Masters.

We saw Tiger make an eagle on thirteen—fist-pump and everything—and then his drive up the fourteenth went right into the rough near us. There was a work cart nearby, so I climbed up the back and then got yelled at by course personnel and told to climb down. That's just me, always getting in trouble wherever I go.

I climbed down from the cart sheepishly, walked about ten paces, and then slid underneath a bush. The bush was large and was a canopy kind of thing, so I was able to hide inside it completely, while also getting right up behind Tiger's ball. I had to peer through some leaves, but no one had a better vantage point than I did for this shot.

The Masters is this oddly polite, well-oiled machine. It's staffed entirely by volunteers, but everyone working there acts like they are being paid $30/hour. Chipper, friendly, informative.

There are open-ended barns for food, usually four lines per barn. The options are simple, but nothing is overpriced. You can spend a dollar or two on a sandwich, another buck for a tea or lemonade. And it's not fine-dining, but everything tastes great.

There are rules at the Masters. You aren't allowed to run. No running. I got a warning when I was running the first morning, even though I was running toward a trash can so I could vomit inside it instead of out in the open. I think it was leftover travel anxiety, but the point is, I still got a warning for running.

After a warning, you get a punch on your badge. And if you get three punches on the badge, you are expelled from the event like a naughty student. I saw a guy get a punch behind the sixteenth tee because, after Tiger hit, the guy yelled, "You're the man!" Boom, staff descended upon him and properly sanctioned his antics.

You can also only buy Masters merchandise *at* the Masters. And we all wanted a shirt or a mug or something to remember the event by. And they have a massive gift shop, with the slickest setup where after you buy your items, you have the option to get in a second line for FedEx and have your merch boxed up and sent to your home no later than a day or two after you yourself get back.

If you're a golf fan, the Masters is a must-see. It's like the

Grand Canyon or the redwoods but for sports. You just have to see it to fully understand the magic.

On the last day, at the last green, as we crowded around the already-crowded eighteenth hole, I nudged my brother and pointed out that our dad was on his tiptoes, hoping to see over the crowd to catch a glimpse of the final putt. That image made the whole trip worthwhile.

And none of it would have been possible if our YouTube channel hadn't taken off.

C2E2

The year 2015 was maybe one of the biggest years for travel for me ever. Shortly after I got back from the Masters, it was time to head off to Chicago for C2E2 in April.

At this point, our friend (and now coworker) Barrett still lived in Chicago, so we met up with him for most of our shenanigans.

C2E2 was crazy on its own. We had one panel scheduled, and we hoped maybe one hundred people would show up, but we ended up turning people away from an eight-hundred-seat room, and that was a fucking trip, man.

We answered questions for an hour, then got surrounded outside in the hallway, and I nearly passed out from panic, but we made it through. And it was a thrill to be treated like celebrities, like people folks would want to know or meet. Strange, but awesome.

We went to dinner at this place that does Wisconsin-style butter burgers, and in addition to a butter burger and fries, I also had a flight of wine. Actually I had two flights of wine. For the uninitiated, a "flight" is a tasting, usually three to five varieties of a thing. You can get a flight of beers, a flight of cheese, and even a flight of whiskey if you to go a really good bar.

Anyway, flights are usually smaller portions, but at four per flight and two flights ... I was drunk pretty quickly. This trip was notable for me as the time I learned of the dangers of combining Xanax and lots of alcohol—which is to say, memory loss.

I left my hotel room five times, racked up two separate bills at the bar downstairs, walked six total blocks, called my wife, and somehow ordered a steak that seemed to just appear on my lap in a Styrofoam container ... all things I can prove happened but which I have no memory of.

I even called my wife in the morning in a panic, apologizing for not having called her the night before like I'd promised to ... only to have her say, "Uh, no, yeah, you *did* call me, you moron."

My doctor told me on my next visit not to mix Xanax and alcohol ever again, and I haven't. It's a devastating feeling to completely lose time—to know for sure you made certain movements and took certain actions but have no memory of any off it.

NYC BookCon

In May of the same year we went to New York City for Book-Con. It was my first ever visit to the Big Apple, and I was giddy. I could even see the entirety of Manhattan Island from the air as our plane circled and descended!

We ended up staying in Times Square. Don't ever do that. Don't stay in any hotel in New York City that is tall. Times Square hotels are built up not out, so it's forty-four floors with five rooms per floor and a fifteen-minute wait for the elevator no matter the circumstances. It's the worst, and the elevators take longer than my adolescence.

Anyway, we still managed to see the new 1 World Trade building, the WTC memorial, Central Park, the Central Park Zoo, and the New York City Public Library. All inside three days! Not bad, if I do say so myself.

One thing we made sure to do while in town was to eat at Craft, the NYC original location of the Tom Colicchio's farm-to-table award-winning restaurant we'd been so wowed by in Los Angeles. The NYC version was just as impressive—I remember our manager, Kevin, ordered rabbit wrapped in rabbit. It had a fancier name, but I only remember that it was rabbit wrapped in rabbit, and it looked like he was eating golden love.

I ended up thinking Bryant Park was the best spot in the city. Granted, the first time I left the hotel, I found a business park with benches four doors down from the hotel, so I sat there and smoked a cigarette until—you guessed it—I got yelled at for smoking, because that particular small business park was a non-smoking area. So I walked further down the block and found Bryant Park the next block over.

Now, Central Park is cool. It's huge. It's an oasis in the middle of a massive metropolitan area.

But it's almost too big. You can get so deep in there that you really do forget you're in the middle of a massive city. At times it felt like the woods out behind my friend Ben's house in elementary school back in Indiana.

Bryant Park is half a block, and that's it. All the buildings nearby are visible. All the traffic flows by, horn honks and all. And yet, there's something serene and quiet about Bryant Park—known mostly for bocce ball, chess, ping-pong, and summer movies on the lawn—that Central Park can't touch. It's maybe that you can SEE the hustle and bustle passing you by, even while you're cozy and quiet in this tiny little park. I ended up going there every single day, just to have a coffee or a tea and enjoy the peacefulness.

BookCon itself was odd. We were there, presumably, to try and promote my self-published book, *The Ables*. But CinemaSins also had a panel scheduled. And way more people turned out for the CinemaSins panel than did for my book signing, which was fine. I was happy to be signing books. But I'm not sure we did much to ultimately promote the books at this event.

The final night in NYC, my wife and I ate at Koi, just off Bryant Park. It was a Japanese sushi and hibachi place, but fine dining and super fancy. Everything was good. But the dessert we ordered, chocolate banana eggrolls, was mic-drop worthy. All I wanted to do for the next hour after eating them was tell everyone I knew in the world about their existence. Holy God on high they were amazing.

We got to have some authentic New York pizza as well as some delicious Hell's Kitchen empanadas. The subway stayed on time, and we hated our hotel. Overall, not a bad trip to NYC.

LA for *Movie Fights*, *Schmoes Know Show*, and a *Nerdist Show* Appearance

Later that summer we took one final 2015 trip, and that was the one that finally drained all the energy from my body. Back to Los Angeles.

Hey, you know how they say it never rains in Los Angeles? Well, it has rained every single time I've ever been to Los Angeles. Make of that what you will.

This time we were out for several appearances, and the schedule was tight.

We appeared on the *Schmoes Know Movie Show*. They had already begun their now-famous trivia show but still had a weekly video show about movies. And we were the guests. We talked about the CinemaSins channel and told the story, and I tried to pimp the book a little bit.

We actually had trouble finding their studio at first, because it's in the back of a house that hosts another studio in front. So we sat in a waiting room for thirty minutes chatting up this actor guy and his girlfriend who was going to be a guest ... on some other totally different show. He was *super* serious about his craft, and that's laudable even if he'd never been in a movie I had heard of. Hey, he'd never heard of us either, so fair's fair.

Eventually a Schmoes person found us and took us back to the correct waiting room, and everything went great from there.

We also swung by the Nerdist studios for a quick segment on the news show with Jessica Chobot. She was super nice, very welcoming, and spoke highly of us on camera to her audience. We also got a mention for my *Ables* novel on that appearance as well.

We were bummed not to meet Chris Hardwick, head Nerdist guy, but we did get a kick out of their OG original *Star Wars* poster hanging in the waiting room. Like, there's what most of you think is the OG *Star Wars* poster, then there's the real OG *Star Wars* poster the majority of the public never saw, and that's the one they had, and it was awesome!

Finally we went to the Screen Junkies studios for an episode of *Movie Fights* that we won, even though history says we lost.

Movie Fights was a popular show on ScreenJunkies's You-Tube channel where known film fans and pundits debate their favorite movies and moments, and a judge awards points to the best arguers.

Our judge was Kristian Harloff, who'd just had us on his *Schmoes Know* show, so we figured he would be harder on us than usual, to avoid any appearance of bias.

Most of the Movie Fight was fine. But the specific question of "best movie car chase" ended in controversy.

Chris and I chose *The French Connection*. It's known for its car chases and for pioneering street-level camerawork and for shooting much of its chase footage without having obtained the proper permits from the Chicago government.

Our Movie Fight opponents offered up *The Matrix Reloaded*. And while *The Matrix Reloaded* has a great chase scene, it is in no way the best car chase ever. And yet our opponents were able to sway the judge by reminding him that the production for *Reloaded* built the entire highway set from scratch just to shoot the scene.

And that is an incredible fact, and it is worth every fan knowing. They built that fucking highway just so they could shoot that sequence. That's amazing.

But building an elaborate *set* does not make the scene in question *better* than another movie's car chase where extensive sets were *not* built. The question is about the car chase, not the set design!

Anyway, we lose that point, I go nuts and tell the judge he's going to have to live with that decision for forever, and finally our LA trip's obligations are done.

But one more trip obligation remained, so we returned to Craft in Century City again. This time we were taking our manager, Kevin, for his first visit. We will never go to LA without dining at Craft.

Craft in LA or New York is going to cost you about $100 per person, on average. But if you can save that up, and you're going to be in either town, you cannot have a bad meal at Craft, I guarantee it.**

**the guarantee stated in the previous paragraph was colloquial and fanciful and does not constitute a real guarantee

CHAPTER 13

Surprises and Accidents and Dumb Luck

The Holy Spirit works in mysterious ways. Sometimes what works really well in a worship service one week totally flops the next week.

Sometimes a service you thought was a filler week ends up reaching people and turning into an extended service of altar calls, heartfelt testimonies, and new recruits.

As a preacher's kid, I'd seen all kinds of services. And I knew enough to know that nothing was predictable when it came to the Holy Spirit.

When Dad repeated what had worked before, either in topic of sermon or type of hymn sung, the results never matched or even came close.

I was such a preacher's kid that there were a few evangelists whose sermons I'd heard more than once. Three and four times even for a few. And they always played differently with the crowd.

I assumed it depended on the people, and the day and time ... the weather maybe. It's like in *Groundhog Day*, when Phil tries to recreate the snowball fight moment, and it feels a little off. Sometimes even a good idea can have a bad landing.

The point is that a lot of intentional planning is undone by the basic unpredictability of human nature. The best laid plans of mice and men and all that.

The Singer

But a lot of pleasant surprises and happy accidents can happen in church too. I remember a man at one of our churches who nearly never spoke. I had heard him say maybe ten words in five years. Just the quietest man you ever met. Big-ass man, too; 6'2" easy, 250 pounds. of mostly muscle. And one day, after an unexpected cancellation from a guest singer, this man wound up on stage about to sing a solo to the whole congregation.

And my face wrinkled in curiosity. I was a teenager, so naturally I was skeptical this would be any good and was already looking forward to talking with friends about how bad it was after the service was over. I smelled a train wreck, like that time I'd tried to sing "The First Noel"—no, you cannot hear the tapes because I burned them long ago.

But instead, when he opened his mouth, this fellow had the voice of an angel, or at least a reality competition winner. No one knew where it came from, and it was thoroughly unexpected by all but his family who already knew about it.

The Smart Kids

There's the time we moved, yet again, in the middle of my four high school years. I'd already done two years, and now we had to move. We moved a lot, and I hated it. It's the nature of the job, so I don't really blame my parents, but moving so often probably wasn't very good for my personal overall mental health.

This particular move, though, came with a silver lining, once I settled in. By some happy accident, in this new school, the smart kids were popular. This was an anomaly for me. I'm no smarter than the average good student, but I made good grades and sometimes ended up in AP classes. All through my life, being a smart kid had been something that got me picked on. But at the new high school, it was a badge of honor.

Certainly the athletes were popular like at any other school, but so were the nerds. I only had two years of high school left, but I made friends quickly and easily. It was nice to know I could walk down the hall and not get picked on because I liked math.

I still only ever got invited to one party. I just never heard about them until they were over. No one ever asked me to go. Finally, I got invited to the post-graduation party, and I went. And when I asked why I had never been invited before, I was told it was because my dad was a preacher. They figured I wouldn't be allowed to go to the parties because there was usually alcohol.

And I'll be honest, my father would have been furious if he knew I'd gone to a party where there was underage drinking—rightly so, since it was, after all, against the law. But I was still a bit let down to know that my family ties had caused an assumption that ultimately kept me on the periphery of the core friend group.

The Lucky Guesses

I mentioned earlier my illustrious career as a teen Bible Quizzer, and how I would memorize an entire book of the Bible for a season of competition. The higher you go in competitive Bible Quizzing, the tougher it gets. People start jumping with answers after only a few words of a question have even been read. I did this myself. I did it at the national level, but I also did it at the local level, where the competition was much weaker, because I was an asshole.

Anyway, when you have all of the book of Matthew memorized, there are some phrase combinations that only appear in a few places. On more than one occasion I jumped to answer without knowing what the question would be and lucked myself into the right answer.

Question: Whom did Jesus tell—

I would jump there. Jesus told a lot of people a lot of things in the book of Matthew. But the language here is also key. The questions were often written with the verbiage from the Bible. So if a verse said "Jesus told Simon to do the hokey pokey," that would be a possible question and answer solution in this moment. But verses that used another verb? "Jesus said to Peter, 'Take video of Simon doing the hokey pokey,'" that could be eliminated.

It was still very often a guessing game, but I was very good at it.

They made it even easier for quizzers like me with the rule of multiples.

Have you ever seen *Quiz Show*, where the contestants will get three-part questions and say something like "I'll take the third part first," or some such?

Multiples in Bible Quizzing is similar to that. If you jump early enough that the question could be finished multiple ways, you are allowed, in the short time allotted for answering, to ask and answer multiple questions. And if the one they were reading is one of the ones you name and answer correctly, then you get the points. But you have to also answer all the other questions correctly.

I know some of you are in the weeds right now as I talk a little inside baseball about quizzing, but I promise anyone that ever did Bible Quizzing is nodding along right now.

Take the Beatitudes. Jesus gives eight blessings during the Sermon on the Mount.

A question might start, "Who did Jesus say are blessed—" And you could jump there.

Then you say "Multiple. Who did Jesus say are blessed because theirs is the kingdom of Heaven? Who did Jesus say are blessed because they'll be comforted? Who did Jesus say are blessed because they'll inherit the Earth? Who did Jesus say are blessed because they'll be filled? Who did Jesus say are blessed because they will see mercy?"

You're probably almost out of time at this point, so you'd just say, "The poor in spirit, those who mourn, the meek, those who hunger and thirst for righteousness, and the merciful," answering all the questions in the right order and correctly.

Then you'd sit down and pray to God one of the five you named was the actual question. Or you talked really superfast and got all eight of them in there.

The Hole In One

Then there's the story of my father's infamous hole in one. And for the record, it's real, and it counts, and I wasn't there to see it, but my brother was.

Par three, 170-some yards ... Dad takes a big swing and tops the ball, sending it rolling along the grass. In high school golf we called those shots worm-burners.

Well, Dad's worm-burner rolls and bounces and skips along 170 yards of grass, leaps up onto the green, and snakes its way into the cup. Hole in one.

I've played golf all my life. When I was young, I was good. I could shape my shots and had a great short game. Played competitively for years. Never even sniffed a hole in one. Dad gets one off one of the lousiest swings in golf history.

———◉———

I'll admit that you don't see quite as many happy accidents in the movie theater industry as you do in church. But there are some.

The Temp

I remember in the mid-'90s, when I was an assistant manager of a three-screen theater, I got a call from the district manager. A theater in the same district, an hour north, needed a fill-in general manager for two weeks while they found a new GM to take the job.

Now, this was distasteful to me for a few reasons. First, I mean ... I'll take the job. If I'm good enough to do it for two weeks, maybe I'm good enough to be the guy you hire full-time, and I can get a big pay raise. But asking me to fill in while you search for a GM? That means I'm out of contention before the search begins. I knew this district manager, and he wasn't going to give me a shot at winning that job full-time.

Second, it's an hour away. I have a true shithole of a car that runs on the will of forces outside my control. And I don't want to lose two hours a day just driving to and from work. Ugh.

Incidentally, do you know *why* they had to hire a new GM? Because the previous one was taking the nightly bank deposits on weekends over to the nearest riverboat casino and gambling all that money! And she did it for two weekends *and* won enough to put the deposit in by the next day, so no one ever knew until she busted out the third weekend. The cops got called when $25,000 didn't end up in the bank when it's supposed to.

Anyway, I'm basically getting used for two weeks as a stopgap, won't be paid any extra, and now I have to drive an hour each way to work.

By the end of that first night, I was making out with the theater's very attractive assistant manager in the manager's office after hours. It might have technically been against company rules, but I figured since I was only a temporary replacement, I wasn't really her boss.

It's amazing how fast anger can melt given the right circumstances.

We made out a few more times during my two weeks, and then we never spoke again. That kind of thing happens a lot in movie theaters, trust me.

The Snowstorm

During the year after I graduated from college, I was living in an apartment with three friends thirty miles north of our college town, Kankakee, IL. Three of us still had jobs in Kankakee and just commuted every day for work.

On one winter night, the snowfall poured on the city, shutting down businesses and a lot of roads. It was icy as well.

Driving back north to our apartment would have been extremely dangerous. So I invited my two friends over to the theater. "Let's just turn on a projector and watch movies all night. I'll even make popcorn." I was, at this point in time, the second in command at the five-screen Paramount theater, still there today, still gorgeous. It's an old, restored theater with one giant auditorium and four smaller, more modern ones.

I couldn't go home, but hey . . . movies!

So one friend arrived with beer and cigarettes—I was a smoker at this point in time, and yes, I do still hate myself for it (I quit more than two years ago, I'm proud to say)—and the other friend brought cigars and snacks.

And we just watched movies all night.

At three or four in the morning, we were in the middle of *The Borrowers*, with John Goodman—it's tiny people living among regular-sized people. We were all buzzed or drunk, smoking, and the door behind us bursts open! "What do you think you're doing?"

It was my boss, the general manager.

I almost panicked, but then he started laughing and put his hand up to his face to take a drag from a cigarette he'd lit before he came in. He asked for a beer and watched the rest of the movie with us.

He lived close to the theater and walked over to see if I'd stuck around and if I was okay. He was a really cool guy, even if I always resented that he was five years younger than me.

People like to believe in and spread conspiracy theories regarding YouTube. Well, people like conspiracies of all kinds, but part of my story is YouTube related, so I'm focusing there for now.

I've heard that CinemaSins pays YouTube in order to get our videos into the top trending list. Still not sure how that computes, math-wise, but it's out there.

I've heard that we scour the IMDb "Goofs" section of a movie to write our sins, which is abjectly hilarious. Go read one of those Goofs sections. Those are the people we are making fun of. Those are the people we get accused of being. You think CinemaSins nitpicks so much they take joy out of movies? Go read the IMDb Goofs. Do it. It will make you cry.

One of my favorite conspiracy theories about CinemaSins is that we started making our videos longer because YouTube had changed its algorithm to value longer videos and longer watch times. And while it's true that YouTube did change their algorithm to give more weight to longer videos, it happened about two years *after* CinemaSins had stretched our average video length from four minutes to twelve.

More recently, YouTube made a decision to value evergreen content over daily-news or quickly devaluing content. This hurt daily vloggers a great deal, as most of their content was current-events based. But YouTube's argument was that current events only mattered for a day or two, and most video viewing was of content that wasn't dated.

The sins videos, by definition, benefited from this shift in YouTube's thinking, as our videos are evergreen and not news-based or about current in-the-moment events. But we still get accused of exploiting some loophole to get on the YouTube Trending list so often.

Another shift YouTube made at one point was to reward higher percentages of video watched. So total watch time was good, but now, so was complete watching. If a person starts a ten-minute video but clicks away after thirty seconds . . . that's bad. But if they watch *all* of a thirty-second video . . . that's good. And because of nothing we did on purpose, our fans and viewers tend to watch our videos to near completion.

There are people who think we are a massive company with dozens of movie-hating employees typing out sins all day long. There are folks who think we are intentionally trying to make people stupid.

Conspiracies are fun. Just remember how many people have to keep completely silent about them for them to ever work for any length of time. And then remember Twitter exists. And people love to be in the spotlight, get on the news, and sell book ideas—including us! ☺

CHAPTER 14

Growth and the Future

Christianity is all about the future. You're either spending it in Hell or in Heaven, and both are rather vivid in your mind, one more than the other, depending on your denomination. The point is, most of us in the church were either raised to have a rabid desire to go to Heaven or a heavy need to not go to Hell ... or both.

It's more important than what you're doing now, because that future is eternal, baby, but it's also DEPENDENT on what you're doing now.

You are either suffering forever or living in luxury forever, and it all hinges on how you act during your brief-ass time as a human being. Sounds fair, right?

In the Christian faith in which I was raised, your past is the past, and no matter how horrible it is, you can still be forgiven and get "right" with God. He is willing to wipe away ALL SINS in exchange for your fealty.

But your future? That was always in doubt, constantly being judged by how you behaved after your confession and forgiveness. Your ledger needed to have more black than red, basically, from a moral standpoint. At least that's how I felt.

I knew the Bible said it was a sin for me to think impure thoughts, but I still thought about sex every time I saw Amy Wagnerson or Steph Goodall (names changed to protect my pride). The Bible also had strong words to say about impure actions, and it seemed worse to act impurely than to merely think about it. So I usually considered myself in the clear if I momentarily pictured Amy Wagnerson naked before deciding not to masturbate.

To hear some Sunday School teachers or preachers tell it, I shouldn't even be having the sexual thoughts in the first place. I vividly remember one teen camp speaker saying "Masturbation is a sin! And some of you may giggle that I said that word, but even *thinking* about masturbation is a sin." I remember thinking, in my own Christianized internal dialogue, "What the fuck, man? How can we NOT think about it if you just said it?! And also, how are you allowed to SAY it if we aren't allowed to THINK it?!"

Not thinking about sex or getting aroused seemed impossible. How could it be my fault I was thinking about sex all the time? How do I try and address that concern if you're telling me I'm evil for even having the sex drive in the first place?

So I'm out there walking around, a horned-up young teenager trying to be like Jesus, praying to God to take my boners away. In hindsight, that's pretty fucked up. Most young teen boys get boners a lot, because, you know, puberty and science.

If I thought about sex or touched myself, I felt guilt for days and would pray for forgiveness. I'd even have emotional breakdowns, crying.

I was always keeping score . . . and if I got red in the ledger, or too much of it, the guilt just fucking happened, man. It poofed right out of thin air. Shame is a terrible thing for a young person to feel over something as natural as sex.

Ultimately, a lot of my time was spent thinking about getting into Heaven and trying to act like the kind of person Jesus would like. I wasn't very consistent at it, or successful, but I tried. I tried like crazy.

The last thing I wanted was to burn in Hell for eternity.

The earliest nightmare I can remember having was about an earthquake. Dad and I were walking, and the ground under us opened up into a gaping gorge, with lava and fire rising up from within it.

And also King Kong, who climbed up to the ridge, grabbed my father, and threw him down into the fire.

I was six years old.

I was also frequently warned about another scary future on par with Hell: failing to get into a good college and get a degree.

For Generation X, which includes me, getting into a good college and getting a college degree was the ticket. Or it seemed like it. The message we received was: get a good degree from a good school and you *will* have a career.

And that's just a fucking lie.

I got straight As in high school. Because of a stupid weighted points system for AP classes, I actually graduated with a GPA that was higher than 4.0. I was third in my class.

I got into a good college, albeit a super-Christian Nazarene university, but it was one with an excellent academic record. And I realized pretty quickly that I wasn't special there. Everyone at that school was a good student. The exceptional ones there in college would be out of my league.

This killed my desire for straight As, which in turn increased the number of times I skipped Spanish class. I ended up graduating with something around a B- or C+ average, with a BA in speech communications . . . whatever that is.

I never used it.

I went to work as an assistant movie theater manager while I was still in college. By the time I graduated, I was making $22,000 a year.

I worked as a theater manager for a year or two before my roommates and I decided to move to Nashville. A few friends and I had all visited Nashville before, and there were friends and relatives there for most of us. So we packed it up and moved in late 1998.

For a while I assistant-managed a Blockbuster video before I finally got hired in April of 1999 at the Regal Cinemas Hollywood 27 at the 100 Oaks Mall just south of downtown Nashville.

I stayed with Regal until 2003, when I had finally had enough of the late hours and poor corporate support, and I quit. I temped for a while and did some graphic design freelance work. But when finances got tight, I took the only job I was qualified for: retail manager. This time it was Kroger instead of a movie theater.

Please make note of the fact that I really still haven't used my speech communications degree at all to this point, at least for career purposes.

Kroger turned out to be the most stressful job ever, alongside some of the nicest people I've ever met. I was both sad and relieved to say goodbye to grocery management inside of ten months after I'd started.

I was hired on faith by a web development firm that wanted to get into the search engine optimization game to help clients rank better on Google. They hired me to learn the craft quickly and start using it for client websites. This was literally the best job I ever had where I was not the boss—amazing people and interesting work, and I still keep in touch with them to this day.

I did a little bit of consulting work after that, making and marketing videos for small businesses, but at this point Chris and I were actively creating YouTube videos and channels, and within a few months, CinemaSins took off, and I dropped everything else.

But I had still spent tens of thousands of dollars on a college education that never advanced my career. And I did fine, really, without it.

If I had teenagers today, I would *not* send them to college. I might send them to a trade school or tell them to learn something they enjoy doing by watching YouTube videos. That same school I went to twenty-five years ago? It's nearly $50,000 a year these days. I would never send my kid there when Tennessee community colleges are 100 percent free to Tennessee residents.

In the cinema management business, there is no future. Not for most. I was fortunate to ascend from assistant manager to general manager, but I was one of the lucky ones. Even fewer still go from GM to district manager.

The truth is that most theater assistant managers never advance beyond assistant manager. It's a field where movie-loving people go to make thirty grand a year for the rest of their lives until they die in poverty.

Hell, there's an assistant manager at my local theater who worked under me as an assistant manager when I was GM there eighteen years ago. And I'm sure he's making good money, because you do get raises if your performance is good. But he's never been given a shot at being the GM of a theater. Just a perpetual assistant. It's a very common story. Very. Especially after the downsizing that occurred in the early 2000s when theaters realized exactly how badly they'd oversaturated the market with cineplexes.

And if you do manage to make it to general manager, it's not the paradise you always believed it was. In fact, it's a little bit hell.

Okay ... it's a lot hell.

You're constantly being judged by and sent instructions from multiple superiors, including your district manager and several home-office employees from HR, booking, concessions, and more.

You're also not paid that much more than an assistant manager. You are, instead, given a "bonus" as a larger raise. But the bonus is this convoluted equation Will Hunting himself couldn't solve that factors in everything from attendance to payroll costs to inventory losses. A lot of these factors were out of my control, yet my ultimate pay was being determined by them.

More often than not, I didn't get a monthly bonus, and when I did, it was small.

The future of CinemaSins is, we think, pretty bright. YouTube continues to be a volatile place to do business, so we have tried to diversify our outputs and incomes.

We hired our friend, Barrett, to help write the scripts for our MusicVideoSins channel almost as soon as we launched it. Barrett lived in Chicago at the time, but our needs didn't require him to be local to Nashville, and he was our friend and we trusted him, *and* he had an utterly massive knowledge of music and music history.

It wasn't long before Barrett started urging us to do a podcast. It was mid-2014, and podcasts were all over the place, but Chris and I had yet to really conceive of ourselves as podcasters.

We were also busy writing scripts for videos.

I remember telling Barrett, who was quite persistent, "I'll do a podcast when all I have to do is show up and talk for however long, and everything else from editing to marketing to ad sales is done by someone that's not me."

Not long after, in December of 2015, we launched our podcast.

We didn't miss a single week for five years, which doesn't probably get enough credit, even though all of it should go to Barrett. He plans the show topics, records the show, acts as cohost, then edits the episodes, and he deals with all the advertisers and distributors!

We have several related channels on YouTube, including MusicVideoSins, TVSins, a channel for our *SinCast* podcast audio, and a CinemaSins Jeremy channel where I post stupid videos of me playing video games while drunk. But that's five channels with a combined YouTube subscriber base well over eleven million.

And we've expanded into other areas as well. We have a merch store that supplies our hardcore fans with wearable CinemaSins gear.

And we've gone full audio as well. Today we have our main podcast, the *SinCast*. We have regular minipod movie reviews from two or more of our sin writers. We also have a podcast about HBO's *Barry* and a podcast about music called *50/50* from Barrett and our good friend Mike. Our lovable employees, Jonathan, Aaron, and Deneé, also have a podcast called *Behind the Sins*, about what it's like to write sins videos and work for CinemaSins.

We have a Patreon, where members of all levels get all our content early, before the general public, and other tiers get access to monthly live-broadcast video hangouts or voting capabilities on future sins videos.

So . . .

Where do we go from here? This is a serious question we're asking ourselves as a company, but also a reference to the glorious musical episode of *Buffy the Vampire Slayer*.

As of this book's first publication, we have five YouTube channels, over eleven million subscribers, three full-time podcasts, and a total of six full-time employees trying to make funny shit for people to enjoy.

What about a CinemaSins app?

Good question! We can't figure out a good solution here. Either we do something that allows you to record your own narration and ding, in which case we worry group movie viewings would be ruined by fans of ours using the app when it's not wanted ... or we would do something lame and cash-grabby that doesn't represent what we're about.

What about a fan event? Beat you to it. It's called SinWeek, and it's held in the spring, and we have done two so far, and they are only going to get better and better. Just search Twitter for #Sinweek, and you'll see what I mean.

We're also hopeful about testing some live show ideas, in the hope we could travel the globe and entertain our fans with silly live-sinning or other tomfoolery.

CHAPTER 15

Let's Talk about the Villain's Plan

The Devil is a weird character, from a literary perspective.

He doesn't show up that much in the Bible, actually, but he looms large over much of Protestant American religion. When I was really young, I always pictured a Rumpelstiltskin kind of Devil. Short and hunched, wiry and frail.

South Park: Bigger, Longer & Uncut changed that perception forever.

Whatever he looks like, my question is basically: what is he waiting for? It's been a couple thousand years since his main foe, Jesus, died and grew more powerful than Satan could ever have imagined.

Does dude not have ANY countermoves planned?

Sure, Christians will tell you Satan is active in the world today, using his tricks to manipulate humans into doing terrible things.

But this guy went toe to toe with fucking JESUS, man! Taunted and tempted him, quoted scripture at him. Are you telling me he's doing a long con? He's patient?! You think he's Aaron Burr from *Hamilton*—not standing still, but lying in wait?

Satan has no plan. Yes, the Bible talks a bit about an Antichrist, and maybe that person is alive and well today, perhaps alarmingly in charge of an entire territory or country.

But if the Devil's plan was to sit back and wait for two thousand years, doing only tiny things through minions and demon slaves, waiting for a truly evil person to come along and cloak themselves in Christianity? That's a terrible plan. What a bad plan. This is MacGruber's "see what happens" plan. It's an anti-plan.

And you can't have a good hero without a good villain.

Sometimes villains are hiding in plain sight, posing as heroes.

I remember the first time I learned that preachers weren't perfect. I was in fifth grade, and I overheard my parents talking about another preacher two towns over who had cheated on his wife and gotten his secretary pregnant.

The very idea of it baffled me. I thought preachers were called by God himself. I thought they were already saved and sanctified. If we can't look to their lives for an example of how to live like a Christian, where can we look?

Of course, I now realize how many members of the clergy were sinners. How wrong we laypeople were to deify our pastors and priests. How much of the Bible was warped by the worst of the clergy to cover up or explain away their own terrible deeds.

There was more evidence to come.

I remember the drug-addicted youth pastor, the girl who got pregnant that we never saw again, the surprise sex offender in the choir, and the Sunday School teacher that I'm pretty sure tried to touch my genitals, though he tried to play it off like an accident.

It wasn't just confined to church. In my youth, I saw a principal fired for embezzling, a mayor ousted for an affair, and a president impeached for a blow job.

I saw idols fall all over the place, from Pete Rose to Mike Tyson.

And that kind of shit messes with a kid's head. Finding out your religious hero is a sinner is like finding out Christian Bale isn't American. It may be true, but it takes mountains of evidence before you believe it, and even then it's really hard to recover from.

But we all go through this. Maybe your idols aren't criminals banned from baseball for life or evil horny bastards. But we all have people we had put on a pedestal who've let us down. We all have that moment of realizing, "Oh, right, every human is fallible."

We all realize, at some point, that there is the person we see on the big screen, and then there is the person behind the curtain, pulling levers and pressing buttons.

It's a sobering moment for anyone. It's the first time most of us learn to be truly skeptical.

Growing up in Baltimore, and an Orioles fan, Cal Ripken Jr. was always a hero of mine. And then after he retired, when all those steroid stories came up for various sluggers in the '90s, I kept hoping no one ever brought Cal's name up, because I needed to believe he was as good a guy as I imagined.

Cal hasn't been implicated in the steroid scandal as of the writing of this book (and probably for many years after). But I would never have even considered it if I hadn't already seen idols fall long before him.

———◆———

The villain during my movie theater years was, of course, the home office . . . the corporation. The massive entity creating unnecessary red tape.

When I was a general manager, my district manager was obsessed with the labor costs. Hours billed per day, dollars billed per shift. Every week I'd get an email asking me to lower my payroll for the weekend coming up.

So I would slash hours and cut shifts, but then we'd be over-run by customers and end up short-staffed. That would lead directly to calls to the DM's office as well as negative comment cards. So next I'd get an email or a call from my boss telling me to keep my negative comments down and that customer satisfaction at my theater was low.

I have one story of my time as a movie theater manager that perfectly encapsulates why working for a giant corporation sucks ass. I was managing a ten-screen theater in middle Tennessee. Great employees, relatively wealthy town, few problems. It was a cushy enough job. As long as nothing major went wrong, most bosses up the chain were happy. We had good comment scores and a high percap—dollars spent per customer—and we made more money than we lost.

But my district manager at the time was a hardass. He was intelligent, sarcastic, and really funny, but I hated him. He

believed he couldn't come to a theater for a visit without finding something wrong. He delighted in finding a new something
wrong every time he came out.

Once, he scolded me for dead grass in the parking islands
and demanded I get it green again. So I hired a dude with a
giant water tank to come water the grass every few days, and the
grass grew back, but then I got bitched at about the bills from
the watering guy.

The same district manager once told me to have my assistant manager change his shirt because it was too big. "He's too
skinny for a shirt that big," he said.

Again, this guy had clearly decided that his self-worth came
from pointing out mistakes at theaters under his management.
So I came to expect it. No amount of cleaning or preparation
would help me avoid him finding problems with my theater. He
was a heat-seeking missile made of ice.

I just realized that "heat-seeking missile made of ice" is a
phrase of my own just-now coinage, and also that it's not very
good. It's intended to suggest that, being made of ice, this missile would be attracted to *everything* around it . . . an analogy for
my district manager able to find flaw in any direction he looked.
But ice is not attracted to heat . . . that I'm aware of.

Anyway, I genuinely liked him, but the function of his job
and his enthusiasm for it canceled it out and made me loathe
him.

So, one Friday night, I got a call from my district manager.
Let's call him Bart, shall we? It was 9:30.

"Why aren't you at your theater on a Friday night?" he
growled.

"I got there at 11:00 a.m. and opened and stayed until eight after the seven o'clock shows were all running," I replied calmly.

"Oh." Every now and then I stumped him. "Do you have any idea what that idiot Craig is up to?"

Craig (not his actual name) was one of my assistants. He was fine. He wasn't exceptional, and he wasn't terrible. But he did have a short fuse for customers screaming at him.

And on this night, one customer had screamed at Craig long enough to make him say, "Why don't you tell it to my district manager?"

The customer, of course, agreed, and Craig went into the office to retrieve Bart's phone number.

Now, in the manager's office, we had a card with important phone number contacts listed. If an ice machine stopped producing ice, there was a number for that. If the popper stopped popping corn, there was a number for that. And for Bart, the district manager, there were three numbers: office, beeper, and home.

I'm sorry, but I have to interrupt here, I feel, to explain that this was in 2002, when both cell phones and beepers were still pretty common, but few folks had both. Anyway . . .

Guess which number our hotheaded Craig gave to the angry customer? That's right, the home number. And that customer was *pissed*, so she went outside and called that shit immediately and WENT OFF.

It's worth noting that Bart had reamed me for not being at work on a Friday night at 9:30 while he himself was home. But let's continue . . .

Anyway, so now between the customer, Craig, and Bart . . .

Bart is the most pissed of all of them, because a screaming customer just called his home number, a number we only had in case of true "someone is dead" emergencies.

"This is what I want you to do," he barked into the phone. "Tomorrow morning you go in there, and you write him up for giving out my home number. He's already got one write-up, so that'll make it two. Then write him up for being rude to a customer, and that'll be the third write-up, and you suspend his ass and take his keys."

Tennessee is a right-to-work state, which makes firings . . . interesting. So all firing was done by corporate employees in HR at the home office, and they consulted with lawyers to determine who was most likely to sue for termination.

The point is, as general manager, I could hire anyone I wanted, but I couldn't fire anyone. I could only "suspend and take keys" and send it in to HR at the home office.

Craig was a middling manager, and I wasn't sorry to see him go, but I did like him as a person. I would not have fired him for this, though part of me would always wonder if he gave out the DM's home phone number on purpose. They'd clashed a few times in the past, and Craig was known to carry a grudge.

Anyway, I did what I was told and took his keys, and he couldn't believe it. He was in shock. I felt awful. He was suspended for two weeks while HR investigated.

Ultimately, HR decided he'd been written up unjustly. Craig was reinstated, keys and everything.

And I got written up by HR for "filing flimsy write-ups." Which I had only done at my boss's direction. When I asked him by phone why I was being written up for doing what he'd told me to do, he said I'd written sloppy reports that would have held up if I had done a better job.

So I did my boss's bidding and ultimately got in trouble with his bosses. That's corporate America. I worked for Regal Cinemas, I worked for Kroger, I worked for Blockbuster, I worked for enough corporations to know that this is how it's done. CYA. Cover Your Ass. Cover your own ass, and do enough to not get in trouble. The rest is up to fate.

The villain of the YouTube/CinemaSins era of our story is the YouTube copyright claim system.

I can tell you firsthand that YouTube and the world of online video and copyright is a mess. The authorities—copyright holders and YouTube itself—can't agree on who's responsible. So it results in YouTube bending the rules to let movie studios and music publishing companies claim anything and everything they want.

Then the channel has to dispute the claim. Then the studio has a chance to double-down on the claim. Then the channel has another chance to dispute the claim with the risk of going to court.

I lost faith in YouTube early on. I think it was the *Dark Knight* sins video. It was blocked and disappeared hours from launching. But then a few hours later, it was back. It was both unnecessary censorship AND oddly fast retraction of said censorship.

At CinemaSins, we take movie footage and add commentary, critique, and parody/humor. We also literally add visual elements over the top of the footage. We clearly meet the criteria for Fair Use of copyrighted content, in that no one would ever confuse our content for the film we are mocking.

But YouTube isn't the US court system. It's weighted heavily against creators and in favor of claimants.

Entire channels have been wiped out through abuse of the copyright system on YouTube. One day, perhaps, the courts will address copyright as it pertains to Fair Use and online video, giving a clear definition everyone can go by. Until then, studios and publishers just keep claiming anything and everything they see even a remote thread of connection to, and in doing so they steal millions in revenue from diligent hardworking video creators.

Before CinemaSins, we were releasing a bunch of supercut videos. One of them was "All the Gear Shifting in the *Fast & Furious* Movies." This was when the popular film series was at four or five films.

And the director of *Fast & Furious* 4-6, Justin Lin, posted our gear-shifting supercut video to his Facebook page! Euphoria! Delight! Hilarity!

Then the video got a takedown notice from Universal, and we had to delete it or lose the channel.

The director of the films was loving and sharing our video, but YouTube's archaic rule system gave some button-pushing platypus at the Universal home office a way to flex and show power, and he or she took it.

That was actually the beginning of the end for that supercut channel. And the birth of CinemaSins, actually, as I distinctly remember telling Chris, "We are going to create a channel that uses movie footage legally if it's the last thing I do, goddammit!"

Just because someone has authority over you does not mean they are right about everything and you are always wrong. Practical authority and intellectual authority are totally separate things.

Another villain we face is the troll. Not just the common troll—hell, you could make an argument that our videos are a form of common trolling. I mean the scary, violent troll. The threatening troll. The one that wants to make you frightened.

In 2015, a series of threatening messages resulted in us hiring security for a couple of public events. I don't want to reward the person that sent them by pasting them into this story, but I think I'm safe saying that death threats over YouTube videos you don't like is going a handful of steps too far.

To be clear: death threats for any reason are a step too far.

The people who hate our videos? I don't consider them villains. In many ways, they represent our own success. We're lucky to have enough success to also have haters. I remember when it suddenly became trendy to hate on Coldplay. I was confused, because their music was good and pretty harmless. And, hey, they still sell out stadiums and make popular records ... but I guess my point is that anything that gets some measure of popularity will also get some measure of hate. I don't like it, but I can't change it. There's probably even someone out there cold enough to hate Tom Hanks.

As far as I can tell, the people that truly hate us, for the most part, don't actually watch our videos. They are making a snap judgment based on our video titles or someone else's anger.

But when I see videos criticizing our own sins videos or

tearing us down, I see that as a sign of our success. We even see a distinct rise in subscriber rate every time a video like that comes out, meaning they are sending as much new business to us as they are creating for themselves.

I wish we had fewer haters, but we have tons of fans, so I try to take it all in stride.

At the end of the day, we are playing a character, written by six people, who obsessively judges and nitpicks movies in a series of YouTube videos that millions of people enjoy and understand.

And that's enough for me.

CHAPTER 16

It Stays with You

I remember a lot of things from my religious upbringing. Some are Bible verses. Some are songs. Some are kind Sunday School teachers.

The music is really what I remember most, if I'm honest. Some of the scripture has faded with time, but I still know most of the songs. I still know the melodies and lyrics.

Music was always my favorite part about Christianity. It was . . . expressive . . . shared . . . communal yet personal.

No single song sticks out in my memory more than "Thank You Lord." We rarely sang it in church. But my father would sing it to me nightly upon tucking me in.

> *Thank you, Lord, for saving my soul*
> *Thank you, Lord, for making me whole.*
> *Thank you, Lord, for giving to me . . .*
> *Thy great salvation so full and free.*

Even today I get chills just thinking about this song; that's how great a comfort it became to me as a young child. My dad wasn't a world-class singer, but he could mostly stay close to the pitch. And knowing he was singing to God, asking him to help calm me always seemed to work.

Even while writing this book I had to look up some scripture on Google because I had forgotten it. But it seems most of the songs are still in my brain. I could sing "Wonderful Grace of Jesus" right now. Or "Amazing Grace." Or "Love Lifted Me." "It Is Well with My Soul!" "How Great Thou Art!"

I miss the music so much. Looking back, it was really the final thread keeping me tied to the religious life. Most of the theology had rung hollow for me for years, even though I wanted to believe if only to please my father.

But certain stories in the Bible always stood out to me as funky.

Like God asking Abraham to sacrifice his son.

Or flooding the entire world because you're mad at general human behavior.

Or letting your beloved children burn in Hell forever because they didn't say the right words and follow the right rules.

Or . . . Leviticus!

But no matter how much I embrace a more empirical and science-based life philosophy, I'm still moved by gospel and Christian worship music whenever I hear it. I still respect and admire everyone I know that still practices their faith. It just . . . stopped working for me.

It stopped dead in its tracks.

Movie Watching

I still can't watch a movie without critiquing its presentation. Whether it's the lights or the sound or the focus, I can usually spot something I would have fixed if I were the projectionist.

I'm also spoiled after so many private viewings and preview screenings with minimal guests, so watching a movie in a crowd is an added obstacle, since the general public sucks ass and makes tons of noise and shit.

I can tell when theaters haven't been cleaned between shows. And a sticky floor will definitely bug me for an entire film and ruin my experience.

I can tell when the projectionist is late in starting his shows. I can't do anything about it, but I usually silently curse him or her.

I can hear every blown speaker, and I see even the tiniest masking error. And let me tell you, most theaters today don't give a shit about masking whatsoever. But I notice, and it bothers me every time, dammit!

I'm also tainted forever on some of the concession products. I know how long a theater can keep a cooked hot dog on site for sale before having to throw it away. I know what the nacho cheese is made of.

And even though theaters have upgraded their concession offerings these days, I have no more confidence about the burgers and wings than I do the hot dogs.

Food Safety

After I left the movie theater business, I spent a brief time in marketing, and then I landed in the management training program for Kroger. This program lasts six months, sends you to several stores for various trainings, and is known to be one of the top training programs in the country.

I definitely learned a lot.

For instance, if you want Kroger to make money, buy their spices. That's the highest mark-up item that they sell. It's obscene how marked up the dried spices and herbs are.

I also learned that every product on every endcap and shelf is there for a reason, and that reason has tons of market research behind it. So if you find your favorite item has moved locations or been discontinued . . . thank your fellow shoppers, who gave the data to Kroger that suggested the change.

I also had to train to become a certified food safety inspector. So I did.

This was mostly because grocery stores are sometimes hit with surprise health inspections, and if the managers are all trained to do those inspections, we should be able to train early and get the jump on any issues.

I still have the card that certifies me as a food safety inspector, but it's out of date. The point is that I spot food safety violations out in public all the time. It's frightening, actually.

Next time you're at a restaurant, look at the ice machine. Do they have the scoop inside the machine with the ice? That's a food safety violation.

Is there raw meat stored near or above cooked food? That's a food safety violation.

I can't shake it. It's in my blood. There are even a few restaurants my wife and I don't patronize because I saw too many violations. It's like that *Friends* episode where Phoebe dates a health inspector, and he shuts down all her favorite spots. I'm that guy, but without the power to actually shut places down.

Lawsuits

Two years after I'd left the theater management profession, I was contacted by a lawyer to give a deposition in a lawsuit against my former employer, a leading theater chain.

And while I had no love for my former corporate overlords, I had even less respect for the disingenuous argument being put forth by the plaintiff's attorneys.

And don't worry, I never signed anything that said I couldn't talk about this—just another failing in the system, if you ask me. I'm leaving out names of people and companies just to be on the safe side. But the company, at least, rhymes with Shmegal Shminemas.

Anyway, the issue at hand was a woman who had fallen inside a theater I was managing. This wasn't a stadium seating theater—this was back in 2002 before everything went stadium and luxury. We had slope seating, which still gave everyone a good view without having to use stairs.

Behind the last row of seats was a carpeted wall to dampen sound and just enough space for an average-sized person to wiggle through. This provided managers and ushers a way to get from one side of the auditorium to the other without having to cross in the middle of a row of customers, making them all stand up, but also not having to go out the door into the hallway and down to the other auditorium door.

So for some reason, this lady decided to walk back there to get to the other walkway on the other side, and she slipped on a roll of carpet. We were in the midst of having our carpet replaced, and the overnight crew would roll up unused carpet and stash it behind the last row in various auditoriums for easy access the next night of work.

So she fell. She hurt her hip, and a necklace broke. I remember being at work this day and filling out the insurance accident report. In fact, the only reason I was called to give a deposition in the lawsuit was because of my signature on that report.

And look. Maybe most movie theater managers aren't great debaters. Maybe they're ready to turn on their former employer or just too dumb to see the train coming.

But this lawyer for the woman who fell, he kept hammering the phrase "reasonable to assume." Over and over and over. He kept trying to get me to repeat it back to him—I guess he had no idea how stubborn I was.

"Isn't it reasonable to assume a customer might wander back behind those seats?" he asked.

"No," I answered.

"Is it reasonable to assume customers saw you and your employees back there?" Same question, different details. I was aware of the repeated verbiage, and it struck me as important.

"I make no assumptions about movie theater customers, except that they are likely almost always looking at the screen."

He cleared his throat. "No one ever saw you back there?"

"I didn't say that."

"So it's reasonable to assume, then, that someone saw you?"

"You clearly want me to agree to or say the phrase 'reasonable to assume,' so I'm guessing it's a big legal bugaboo phrase that helps you win your case, due to precedent and such. But what if

I don't want to say your phrase?" I was openly challenging him, and I'm honestly surprised he didn't dismiss me right then.

"Isn't it reasonable to assume," he replied, undaunted, "that if a customer saw you or your employees behind the last row of seats, that it was a safe place to walk for customers?"

Eventually I lost my patience. "Look, customers see me in the office, in the stock room, behind the concessions counter, up in the projection booth, and even on the goddamn roof . . . but none of those sightings cause the customer to believe they have a right to step into the areas where they saw me!"

At lunch, the theater chain lawyer grabbed my arm and whispered into my ear: "They never saw you coming. You just won this case for us."

And look, I didn't go into it wanting to win the case for my old employer. I actually hated my old employer. But when someone tries to trick me to get me to do or say something they want, I become more stubborn than a honey badger. Once I realized this guy thought he could trick me into using a phrase that would help him in court, I was ready to burn the world to the ground rather than give him what he wanted.

The sin-writing stays with you as well. At least if you do it professionally. You put on that hat so many times, and it's inevitable you will eventually forget to take it off.

Sometimes I find myself live-sinning a show my wife is watching.

"She's not a therapist! Why are they listening to her? Why did they give her a show?"

Sometimes I find myself live-sinning the shows I'm watching on my own.

"Lady, what are you doing going in there by yourself after the dead body you just saw?"

This is not to say all shows and movies are ruined. Not at all. In fact, the more you write for a sins channel, the more you begin to appreciate the stuff that doesn't actually have a lot of tropes and clichés, like *Breaking Bad*, *Knives Out*, or *Pulp Fiction*.

CHAPTER 17

Stories That Didn't Fit in Any Other Chapter

You Were Meant for Me

I remember Jewel came in to see *Gladiator*, along with her rodeo boyfriend.

Our ticket gal committed the cardinal sin of asking if Jewel was Jewel, and her boyfriend went off, dismissing and insulting our ticket gal. I was standing right there, so I don't want to hear it about giving him the benefit of the doubt.

I liked Jewel well enough, as anyone did in the late '90s, but I'll be damned if I was going to let some rodeo guy talk shit to my hardworking employees and get away with it.

So I staged a passive protest. I gathered every usher, manager, and spare worker I could find, so that when Jewel's movie got out, she and her sensitive man-child would have to walk through a SEA of Regal employees standing by.

If you are a celebrity and you want to see a movie in private, there are ways to do this. None of those ways involve smart-mouthing the ticket girl like a douchebag. Maybe he'd had a bad day, sure. Maybe he was tired of fans and media asking about his more-famous-than-him girlfriend (later wife), sure. But treat my employees with respect or I will ... send a super passive-aggressive message.

Converse to that situation is the time I saw Ashley Judd and her race car husband at concessions. It was late at night. Most of the nine o'clock shows had started, but a few were still in previews. And I heard a concession worker next to me take an order. I was only there because I was filling my personal cup with energy-providing Mountain Dew. But I look up and see Ashley freaking Judd looking back at me.

She lifted up her finger to her lips, in the "Shhh" position, smiling.

I said nothing as she and Dario walked down the hall to their movie.

Night Court

One weekend night while closing the twenty-seven-plex, the security guard and I encountered a man sleeping in the top row of an auditorium.

Now, one thing I learned early in theater management was to be careful when waking a sleeping person, because sometimes they go apeshit.

So I went and got one of our security guards, who was a Metro Nashville police officer making extra money as a theater security guard—because we don't pay our police officers enough, and this is true no matter your political views. It's like teachers. We aren't paying them enough, but they are crucial to our society!

Anyway, he and I walked in and turned on the overhead cleaning lights and started up the stairs . . . and the drunk dude woke up.

He saw a cop, panicked, and ran up the stairs, out the rear door, and into the nearest closet he could find.

The officer and I reached the top, went through the door, and both looked at the nearby closet. The officer went through, turned on the light, and . . . the drunk guy was literally peeing all over the place.

And this happened to be our paper records closet. Employment applications and files, work order slips, concession invoices, receipts . . . all being sprayed by urine.

This all occurred just as my district manager—whose office was three doors down—was leaving for the night. And he got very angry about the drunk man peeing on our one-of-a-kind paper records. He called the cops and pressed charges, but he sent *me* downtown to testify against the guy.

And let's be clear . . . at this point in time, the district manager went home to his nice warm bed.

I was seated in the night court room around 2:00 a.m., though it would be awhile before the case I was there for would even be called forward.

There were some bizarre cases. A lot of "drunken such and such." Many of the defendants were accused of doing something while drunk, including my guy!

Eventually I was called forward to testify.

It wasn't a judge; it was a county commissioner or whatever . . . same difference.

"Explain to me what the defendant did," she said.

"Well, he peed on our paper records, ma'am."

"He what?"

"He urinated in a closet that contained all our paper records."

"And you saw him do this?"

"Unfortunately, ma'am, yes I did."

And the crowd went wild.

Standing there listening to the people in the gallery laughing and clapping, I realized how the old sitcom *Night Court* came to be. Because the truly weird shit happens while most of the normal people are sleeping soundly.

Because I was on salary, I got paid nothing extra for spending my night in court.

And the defendant got off with a warning because it was his first public intoxication arrest.

So basically everyone's time got wasted that night except for my district manager.

He Shoots

I only ever had one gun-related incident at a theater I was managing—at least, only one I was on duty for.

I was up in the manager's office, with the GM and a few other assistant managers, when we heard the distinct sound of a gunshot from the main lobby just outside and downstairs from our location. The GM, Mark, and I bolted for the door, leapt down the stairs, and ran out into the lobby like idiots.

Thankfully, it was an accidental firing. Though, if it had been intentional, I have no idea what Mark and I would have done other than probably get shot and die.

How did the gun go off? Well, it fired accidentally when the customer service manager handed the gun back to the man who had checked it prior to his movie.

Yeah. You read that right.

This motherfucker *checked his gun* at customer service, like it was an umbrella. And what's worse, our customer service manager gladly accepted it and stored it in the top drawer with the confiscated fake IDs.

If you're not following the problem: movie theaters do not check firearms. If you have a permit to carry and are in a legal state, you carry. Or you leave it at home. But we do not check them at the front desk like a piece of luggage or a shopping bag. And everyone who should have known so in this instance did not.

Tongue Rock

I was in a Christian rock band through most of college and a few years after.

After university, the band reformed with two new members in northern Georgia.

One of our earliest gigs was a Christian youth coffeehouse. It was the size of a small gymnasium and had a coffee bar, a couch/hangout section, and a main stage at the far end.

Now, in order to play this Christian "club," we had to agree to come to a staff Bible study an hour before the club opened.

No big deal, right? I'd been to a thousand Bible studies. We agreed without hesitation.

So we get there and get let in, and we're sitting in a circle of about thirty people. And the leader guy talks for maybe twenty minutes about—I don't fucking remember, man, he just preached and shit.

Then he says, "Let's all bow our heads for prayer." And so everyone grabs hands and bows their heads, and in about three seconds . . . the entire room erupts in what I can only call gibberish.

They were speaking in tongues, something all of us in the band had never experienced. So all four of our faces went up, eyes wide, staring at each other.

Look, I don't want to crap on people that speak in tongues. Maybe I just don't understand it or don't have enough faith personally. But to me it sounds like gibberish. Granted, I only witnessed it in person the one time.

Anyway, we played our show, and it was awful. We were like the Wonders in their first show with Boss Vick Koss . . . all fumbling and playing in slightly different time signatures because we were all still mildly traumatized by the Bible study that suddenly went Pentecostal on our asses.

False Prophet

When I was in fifth grade, at summer camp, I inadvertently nearly became a cult leader.

The first event was that I was asked to officiate a marriage between two other campers. One was Ben, my friend from back home, and the other was Gwen, a girl from Huntington. They asked me because I was a preacher's kid, and they assumed that I knew how and that I had the authority in God's eyes.

So I faked my way through the marriage of Gwen and Ben, fifteen minutes before lunchtime on Tuesday, the second day of camp.

By that evening, I'd performed another dozen "marriages" and even two divorces.

The next day I was begged to cast demons out of a pet toad, which I accomplished with ease. Also, I had started hearing confession in the dining hall men's room. I sat in the last stall, and confessors took the stall next-to-last.

Let me tell you, that was an eye-opening experience. I learned two of my fellow campers were gay, three were atheist, and that Suzy really super-duper liked Davey.

Somehow, by week's end, I'd become the main religious authority for most of the campers, even above the counselors and the speaker.

I was asked to pray before the all-star softball game, for Pete's sake.

Bad Manager

In its heyday, the Hollywood 27 did tons of business. In the first year I worked there, it wasn't uncommon to see $70,000 or more get deposited after a weekend night.

But an operation that big has lots of cracks.

So this was still in my Christian rock band days, hilariously, and most of our gigs were on Saturday night. However, I was almost always scheduled to work the floor on Saturday night. That meant supervising the ushers and making sure auditoriums got cleaned on time and in the right order.

So, on more than one occasion, I just showed up, worked

an hour or two, then disappeared. I drove to the gig location, changed clothes in the car, and then did the rock and roll gig with my band mates. Then I'd pack up, drive back, changing on the way, and pop back into the theater and start sweeping with the nearest broom and dustpan I could find.

This happened six different weekends and no one *ever* noticed I was gone.

I'm not proud of it, but I'm kind of proud of it.

That's how many managers and employees we used to schedule back when the theater was hopping. Enough so that an entire manager could go missing for three hours and no one would notice.

EPILOGUE

Well, did you learn anything?

No?

I guess that's about right. I don't have many lessons to offer as much as I have stories. Stories I hope were at least mildly entertaining to read.

What are the takeaways I'm hoping you'll find? Well, don't start a YouTube channel. Or, at least, don't start a YouTube channel expecting it to succeed or make you money. Do it for fun, or because you actually want to make videos. But allow me to leave you with one caution: every successful YouTuber I've met is dealing with some kind of anxiety or depression. There is a stress to cranking out content and meeting fan expectations, and anything that gets a little popular will also receive negativity, which isn't always fun or easy to deal with.

What else? Um, don't raise your kid as a preacher's kid ... if you can avoid it. You probably can't avoid it if you already are a preacher. And I'm mostly joking. Being a preacher's kid wasn't always fun, but I do feel like most of my best quality as a person comes from how I was raised, which is to try and think of others before myself.

Um . . . uh . . .

Well, shit. That might be it for the life lessons. Maybe you found another inside these pages, and I'd be happy to hear about it. Just email me at OriginalSinFromPreachersKidToTheCreationOfCinemaSins@ThisIsNotARealEmail.com

But the biggest question is, Did you have a good time reading this tale? Did you crack a smile or maybe even laugh a few times?

Yes? Wait, wait, wait . . .

One at a time please, so I can hear you . . . everyone quiet down! Now . . . did you have fun reading this book?

(puts hands over ears)

I said one at a time, ha ha ha, you rapscallions!

Anyway . . . a sincere thank you, now, for buying his book. My goal was to open up a window into my life and how I came to love movies. Hopefully you feel I've done that.

If not . . . well, shit. I mean, maybe don't buy the sequel? Or give this copy to a library or a Goodwill.

INDEX

ACKNOWLEDGMENTS

Books don't just come out of thin air. Even after a writer has typed or written the book out, there are dozens of people that have an impact on it and help make it come to life. Artists, editors, marketing folks... I will never be able to name them all. But I would like to thank the great people at Turner Publishing, my friends at MadeIn, my CinemaSins family, my business partner Chris, my editor, my wife, my brother, my friends who wrote forwards, and especially my parents.

CPSIA information can be obtained
at www.ICGtesting.com
Printed in the USA
JSHW030725190421
13654JS00005B/2